G000128945

*Communities in Britain*

# The SIKHS in BRITAIN

*Allan de Souza*

B. T. Batsford Ltd, London

# Contents



© Allan de Souza 1986
First published 1986

All rights reserved. No part of this publication may be reproduced, in any form or by any means, without permission from the Publisher

Typeset by Tek-Art Ltd, Kent
and printed in Great Britain by
R J Acford
Chichester, Sussex
for the publishers
B.T. Batsford Ltd
4 Fitzhardinge Street
London W1H 0AH

ISBN 0 7134 5100 9

*For Ravie and Rohan, who remain always before me.*

**Acknowledgments**
A special thank you to the Phull, Ratra and Singh families for their advice, cooperation and friendship. Thanks also to Renate for her support and for typing the manuscript; to the Rai family for their invaluable assistance; and to all those of the Sikh community who have given advice and help. A thank you finally to John Ogle, who has been much more than a photographer and whose assistance has made this book possible.

# Introduction

The word "Sikh" means a seeker of knowledge, and has the added meaning of a "reformer". As seekers, Sikhs gain knowledge and guidance from a guru (teacher or religious leader). The authority of the guru lies not only in the lives of the ten Gurus, the founders of Sikhism, but also in the Sikh holy-book, the *Guru Granth Sahib*, and in the Sikh community itself, the "Guru Panth". We shall look at each in more detail through the course of this book.

Sikhs originate from the state of Panjab in northern India. The Panjab ("Land of the Five Rivers") was once one of the largest, most powerful states. Now it is one of the smallest. Despite forming less than 2 per cent of India's massive population, the Sikhs are an outspoken and important group. However, due to their changing fortunes many have left their homeland and sought their livelihood in other parts of the world. In Britain alone it is estimated that there are a quarter of a million Sikhs.

In their appearance – the man with beard and turban, and the woman wearing the *salwar-kameez* – the Sikhs in Britain are a very prominent and noticeable community. This has made them open to misunderstanding as well as to discrimination and hostility.

The lives and culture of present-day Sikhs are inseparable from their religion and history. If we look, then, at their past we can get a better understanding of the communities today. This book looks at traditional Sikhism as well as the ways in which Sikhs are adapting, either to fit into life in Britain or to make that life fit them. To help in our study we will look more closely at three families: the Phulls in East London, the Ratras in Birmingham and the Singh family in Reading. It is not possible to

The ten Sikh Gurus.

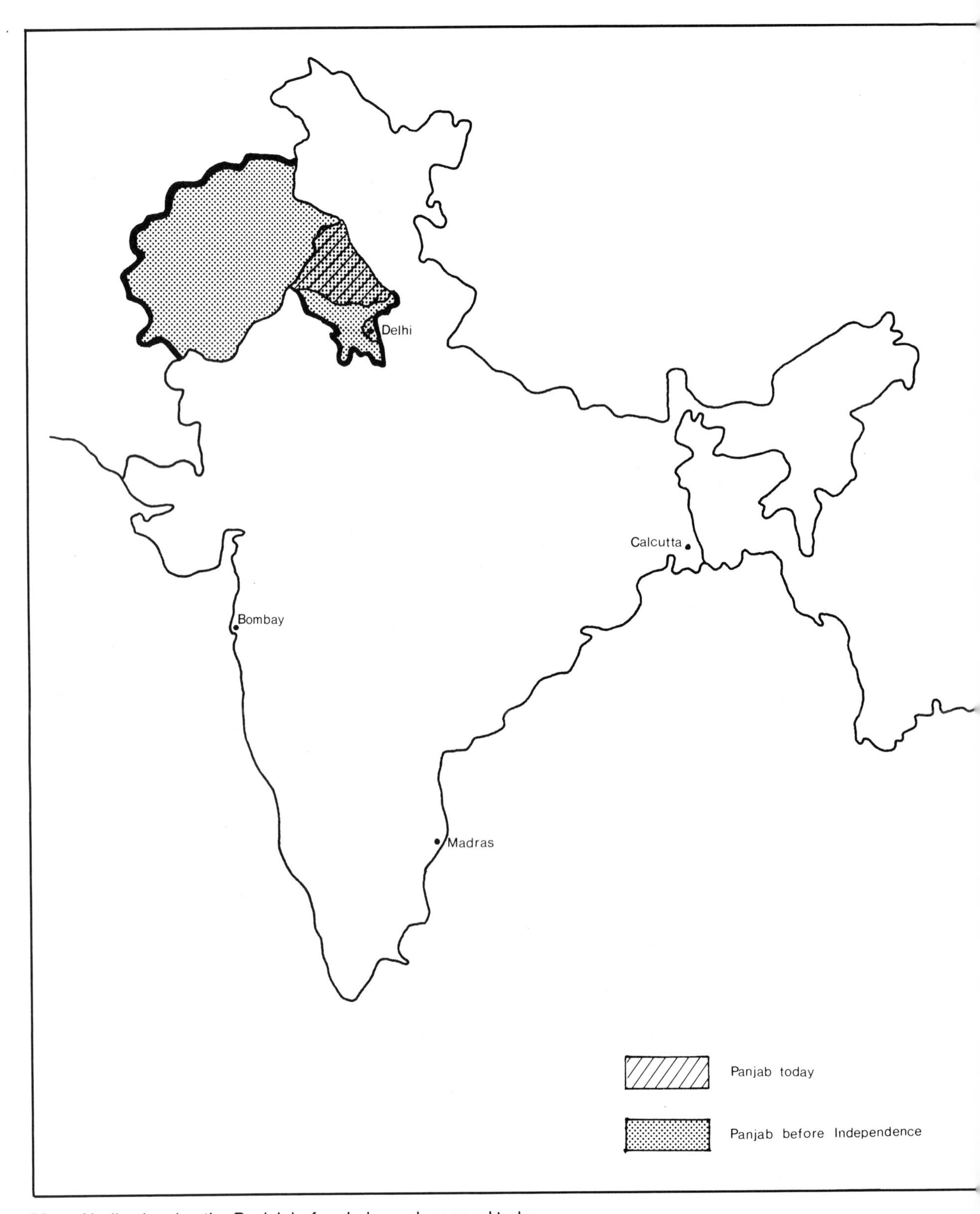


Map of India showing the Panjab before Independence and today.

The Panjab.

give a comprehensive account of the Sikh communities, but through the eyes of these three families we can gain some insight into the depth and variety of Sikh experience in Britain.

Mr and Mrs Phull, 1957. Mrs Phull is wearing *salwar* (trousers) and a *kameez* (top). Covering her head and draped over her shoulders is a *dupatta* (scarf).

The Phull family.

The Ratra family. The two boys, Gurpreet and Kanwardeep, wear their hair tied in a *guthi*, a small knot on top of the head, which is then covered with a *ramal* (cover). During adolescence they will begin wearing a full turban.

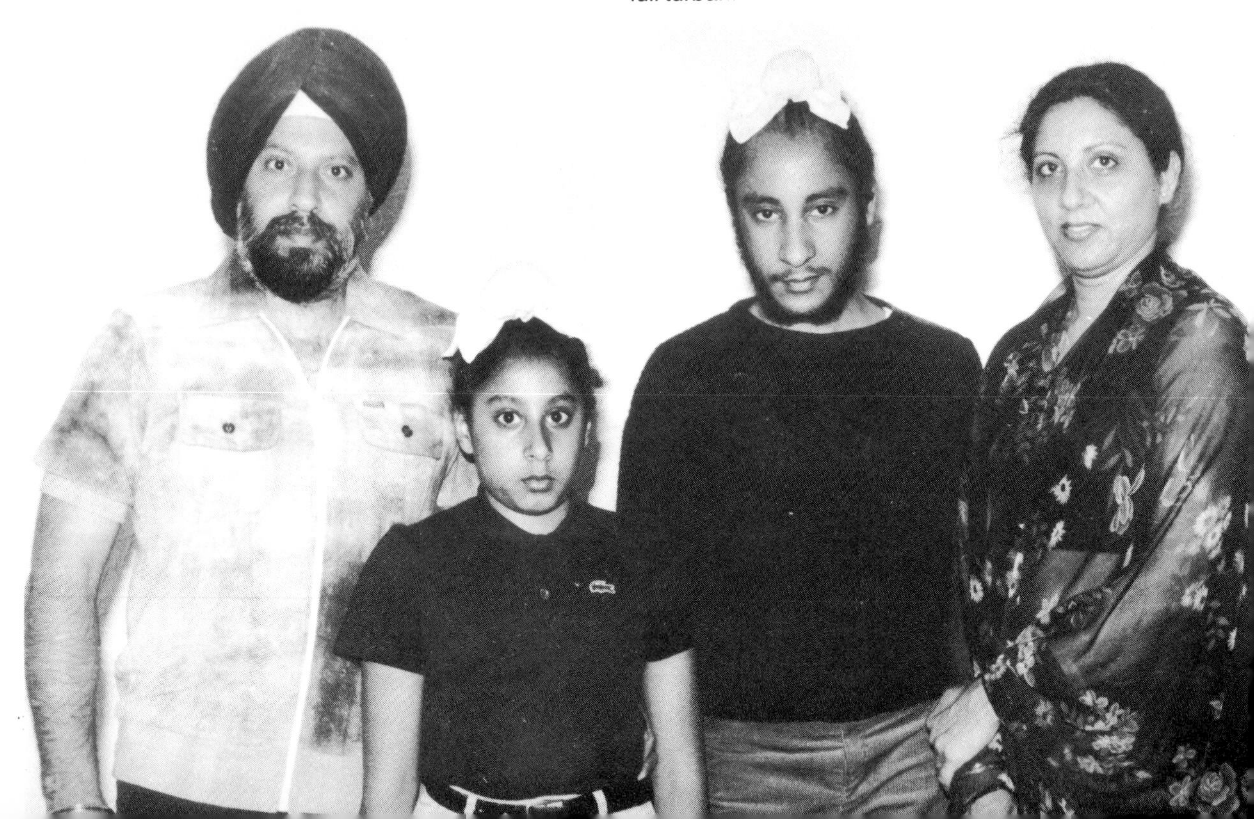

The Singh family.

# 1

# Birth of a People

The fifteenth century in northern India was a period of major political and social unrest. There was an enormous gulf between the rulers and the ruled – that is, the Muslim Mughals and the Hindus. There was widespread looting and destruction of Hindu villages. The people, victims of rape and murder, lived in a constant state of fear. Even among the Hindus themselves there was a rigid caste system, with power and authority wielded by the Brahmin, the priestly caste. The lowest caste, the "Untouchables" were treated as little more than animals. Out of this system of slavery within slavery a number of religious teachers began to appear. The most important among them were Vyasa and Kabir.

As perhaps with all major religions, the origins of Sikhism lie not only with a spiritual relationship with a god, but also in a practical personal life and in the growth of a mass social movement. When Guru Nanak, the founder of Sikhism, was born the seeds of such a movement had already been sown.

## The Gurus

*The founder of Sikhism*

Born in 1469 into a Hindu family, Guru Nanak began to rebel against the caste system and rituals of Hinduism. To him, these were not the way to God but a collection of superstitions and a system of power which benefited the few and oppressed the many. It was not the worship of God, but a political system created by men. He was equally critical of Islam, the religion of the Mughal rulers, because of the fanaticism and intolerance which it preached.

Nanak wanted to find a path which would unite and equalize all the people – rich and poor, ruler and ruled, man and woman, Hindu and Muslim. Moreover, he wanted a religion which would be practical and would offer guidelines for daily life. A religion of love, of brotherhood and sisterhood.

Like other great teachers, Nanak spent a large part of his life travelling and spreading his message. He made four great journeys in his life, travelling north as far as what are now parts of Russia and Tibet; east as far as Assam; south as far as Sri Lanka; and his longest journey, west to Mecca in Saudi Arabia.

His was a message of unity, strength and self-recognition for the poor peoples, and because of this he did not always find favour – his teachings were a threat to the rulers and the power-wielding priestly caste. As a result he was often ridiculed, and even imprisoned.

In his later life, Guru Nanak settled in Kartar Pur (now in Pakistan) working as a farmer. This closeness to the land and the practicality of his life served as a shining example of his teachings. Guru Nanak had always emphasized the importance and merit of manual work.

*The second Guru*

After the death of Guru Nanak, there followed nine more Gurus, each of whom was appointed by his predecessor. Guru Nanak's successor was Guru Angad. He continued the teachings and is best remembered for his contribution towards making knowledge available to everyone. At that time, knowledge and literacy were the prerogative of the powerful Brahmin caste. It was a tool by which they could exercise their power. Guru Angad taught and wrote in Panjabi, the language of the common people, instead of in Sanskrit, which was the

Guru Nanak, the founder of Sikhism.

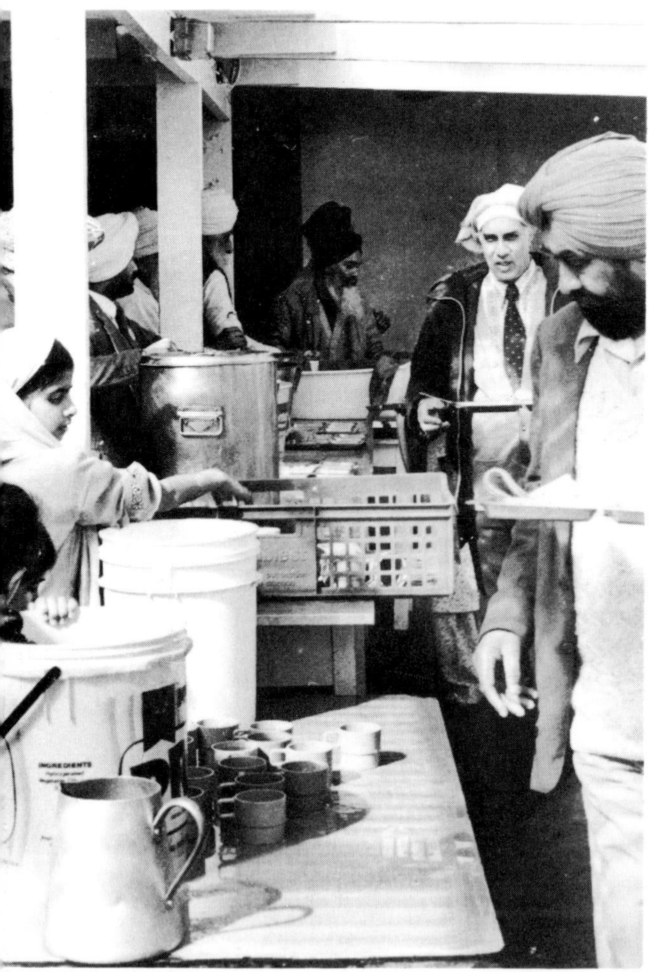
Meals being served at a *langar* in Britain today.

language the priests wrote in. By increasing the knowledge and independence of the people, Guru Angad was able to undermine the authority of the priests.

*The third Guru*
The third Guru, Guru Amar Das, continued the task of educating the people and as a further step towards equality he instituted the *langar* or free kitchen. This meant that every Sikh place of worship would also have a free kitchen service where anyone, regardless of religion, caste or colour could receive a meal. Everyone ate together without any feeling of untouchability or superiority of one person over another. This practice of the *langar* still continues today.

*The fourth Guru*
The Mughal ruler at the time was the Emperor Akbar. He was famed internationally for his progressive attitudes and his tolerance of other religions. In fact, he assembled at his court priests and wise men from every religion. He was so impressed by the Sikhs and their way of life that he presented a large plot of land to the fourth Guru, Guru Ram Das. On this land Ram Das founded the present city of Amritsar ("Pool of Immortal Nectar"), named after its pool of sacred well water.

*The fifth Guru*
His son and successor, Guru Arjun, built the famous Harmandir ("temple for all") in the midst of the sacred pool. As its name suggests, the Harmandir was wide open to everyone and, unlike Hindu temples and Muslim mosques, it had an entrance on each side. Guru Arjun also compiled the *Granth Sahib*, the Sikh holy-book, which was deposited in the temple in 1604.

Under the royal patronage of Emperor Akbar, the Sikh community continued to grow in size and importance. However, with the death of Akbar there was a change of state policy. The new emperor, Jehangir, felt threatened by the increasing popularity of Guru Arjun and vowed either to get rid of him or to convert him to Islam. Jehangir did not wait long: Guru Arjun was accused of aiding a rebellion and was charged with treason. He was tortured and when he refused to undergo conversion to Islam, he was executed.

*The sixth Guru*
The martyrdom of their Guru was a profound shock to the Sikhs and changed them from a peaceful community to one prepared to defend their faith, by force if necessary. They rallied round Guru Arjun's successor, Guru Hargobind, who armed himself with two swords of power – *miri* for worldly strength and *piri* for spiritual might. Similarly he built the Akal Takht, which became the Sikh throne of political authority. It was built facing the Harmandir, so that devotees sitting in the Harmandir could see it and be reminded of their political duties (and vice versa).

From the Akal Takht Guru Hargobind issued a call for his supporters to supply him with horses and weapons and from there he prepared to challenge the

The Akal Takht built by Guru Hargobind as a political and religious throne of authority. Compare this with the photo on p. 63 after "Operation Bluestar", 1984.

imperial might. However, pitted against the much larger Mughal army, Guru Hargobind was driven into the Himalayan foothills, where he remained until his death in 1644.

*The seventh and eighth Gurus*
Before his death, Guru Hargobind chose his grandson, Har Rai, to succeed him. Guru Har Rai's life was relatively undramatic, and before his death he chose his five-year-old son, Hari Krishen, as his successor. Unfortunately, Hari Krishen was stricken with smallpox. Before his death he nominated his grand-uncle, Tegh Bahadur, to be the next Guru.

*The ninth Guru*
Tegh Bahadur was a quiet, retiring man, who did not wish to fight for his rights against a number of others who also claimed to be the new Guru. He founded the town of Anandpur ("Haven of Bliss") where he hoped to find tranquillity and solitude. But, even here, he was not left alone by envious relatives. So he decided to leave the Panjab until the situation had calmed down. He travelled eastwards through Uttar Pradesh, Bengal, and finally to Assam where he remained for three years.

When he returned to his homeland he found the Hindus and the Sikhs in a state of great unrest. The new Mughal emperor, Aurangzeb, had begun to persecute the non-Muslims. Temples were destroyed and both Hindus and Sikhs were forcibly converted to Islam. The Hindus began to look to the Sikhs to protect them. Guru Tegh Bahadur travelled round the Panjab inspiring and giving courage to his people wherever he went.

Once while he was preaching he was approached by a group of Hindu Brahmins from Kashmir. They had been ordered by the emperor to accept conversion to Islam, and so sought the Guru's help. The Guru told them to tell the Mughal officials that only if he, Tegh Bahadur, accepted Islam, would they, too, follow suit.

The Guru was consequently summoned to the Imperial court in Delhi, where he refused to renounce his faith. He was sentenced to death, and beheaded on 11 November, 1675.

Before Guru Tegh Bahadur's decapitated body could be further mutilated and displayed to the public, it was stolen under cover of darkness by one of the Guru's devotees. His son, Gobind Rai, wrote of his father's martyrdom with the words:

> To protect their [the Hindus'] right to wear their caste-marks and sacred threads,
> Did he, in the dark age, perform the supreme sacrifice.

After Emperor Aurangzeb accused him of cowardice for not openly collecting the beheaded body of his father, Gobind Rai replied that he would create a sect "where even one will be recognized in a crowd of a thousand".

*The tenth Guru*
Gobind Rai was only nine when his father was executed, but as he grew up, his mission became

Guru Gobind Singh, who transformed the Sikhs from a pacifist to a martial people.

clearer to him. He wrote: "I came into the world charged with the duty to uphold the right in every place, to destroy sin and evil." Like his grandfather, Guru Hargobind, he also became clearer about the methods open to him to achieve this end. In a letter he later sent to the Mughal Emperor, he declared: "When all other means have failed, it is permissible to draw the sword." It was now time to declare his mission publicly and to take steps to fulfil it. He organized a gathering of all his followers at Anandpur to celebrate the festival of Baisakhi. On the appointed day, a huge crowd gathered. The Guru appeared before them and, drawing his sword, he demanded that five men come forward to be sacrificed. There were murmurings from the crowd, but finally one man stepped forward. The Guru led him to a tent, while the crowd waited expectantly. There was the sound of a sword whistling through the air and slicing through flesh.

The Guru reappeared before the crowd, sword held aloft, but now it was dripping with blood. The Guru asked for another martyr to step forward. The people became restless; a few began to run away, but most stayed where they were, trusting the Guru. Another man stepped forward. He too was led to the tent and the Guru appeared again, with fresh blood on his sword. In this way five men were led into the tent, seemingly to be sacrificed.

Once more the Guru appeared before the crowd, but this time, to the great relief and joy of the crowd, he was accompanied by the five "victims". (The Guru had slaughtered five goats instead.) He announced to the crowd that these "Panj Piyare" ("Five Beloved Ones") would form the core of a new community which he would call the "Khalsa" ("the Pure Ones").

He baptized the five men using *amrit* (sugar mixed in water and stirred with a double-edged sword). They were made to drink out of one bowl to signify that they had joined as brothers in the casteless community of the Khalsa. Their Hindu names were changed and they were given the one family name of "Singh" ("lion"). To demonstrate their equality, the Guru asked the new converts to baptize him into the Khalsa. From then on he became Guru Gobind Singh. To this day all male initiates into the Khalsa are given the name "Singh" and the female initiates are given the name of "Kaur" ("princess").

### The Five Ks

The members of the Khalsa were also given five emblems: *kes, kangha, kach, kara* and *kirpan*. These became known as the "five Ks". *Kes* was the hair and the beard, which were to be left uncut; *kangha* was a comb to keep the hair tidy; *kach* was a pair of breeches, like shorts, which were worn by soldiers at the time; *kara* was a steel bracelet to be always worn on the right wrist; and *kirpan*, a sword to be carried at all times.

The wearing of uncut hair and beard had always been the custom of ascetics and holy-men in India. In proclaiming that his followers do the same, the Guru was creating an army of soldier-saints who would wield weapons only as a last resort, and then only in a righteous cause. The turban itself is not particular to the Sikhs, but is worn all over India by Hindus and Muslims alike. The Sikhs in battle would also wear a metal ring on their turbans, which would act as a helmet and afford greater protection against sword blows. *Kara*, the steel bracelet, performed a similar function in that it protected the right hand which wielded the *kirpan*, whereas the left hand would have been protected by a shield. These "five Ks" became an integral part of the Khalsa identity and are still worn by Sikhs today.

According to Sikh historians 20,000 Sikhs were baptized at Anandpur. This was followed by mass baptisms all over northern India. Soon a new fighting community was born, firmly believing that,

The Khalsa shall rule.
Their enemies will be scattered.
Only they that seek refuge will be saved.

Mr Phull, on far right, newly baptized into the Khalsa community after having received *amrit*. (Kenya, late 1950s).

The Guru now felt ready to resist the persecution of the ruling Mughal regime. He began to prepare the defence of Anandpur against the attack which he knew would come from the Mughal army. He was not to wait long. The Mughals, aided by the local hill chiefs, began their siege of Anandpur. After long and wearisome fighting, the Mughals offered Guru Gobind Singh a safe passage if he would evacuate Anandpur. Realizing that he and his army were heavily outnumbered he accepted their offer.

However he had not gone far when the Mughals, treacherous to their word, came after him in hot pursuit. In the confusion, the Guru's wife was separated from the main party but she was safely escorted to Delhi by a faithful Sikh. The Guru entrusted his mother and two of his sons to a servant, and he continued south with his soldiers. The imperial army eventually caught up with them, and in the resultant fighting the Guru's other two sons were killed, though he himself managed to escape.

While he was regaining strength at Jatpura, he learned that his two remaining sons, Zorawar Singh aged nine, and Fateh Singh aged seven, had been captured and executed by being walled in alive. His own mother had died from shock.

The news of the murders spread rapidly throughout the countryside and thousands of Sikhs flocked to the Guru to help him avenge the crime. While he was building up his army again, the Guru also took time to collect his own writings together and to prepare another edition of the *Granth*, or holy-book. To the Guru it was vitally important that his people should know of their own history.

Soon after, in October 1708, the Guru was fatally stabbed, apparently by Mughal agents. But before he died he called his followers around him. He told them that the line of Gurus was to end with him and, thenceforth, the Sikhs were to look to the *Granth* as their constant guide and as the symbol of the ten living Gurus.

*The development of Sikhism*

The ten Gurus, then, laid down the basis of Sikhism. Under Guru Nanak the Sikhs began as a pacifist people. With continued persecution, they began to change into a people prepared to use force, especially under Guru Hargobind. Later, Guru Gobind Singh, by creating the Khalsa, was to complete this transformation. Yet, although power and strength came to be a vital part of Sikh thinking and of Sikh life,

## Guru Granth

When Guru Arjun, the fifth Guru, compiled the *Granth*, he wrote:

> In this vessel, you will find three things,
> Truth, peace and contemplation.
> . . . Those who partake of this dish and relish it
> Will be saved and emancipated.

At that time the *Granth* contained only the hymns of the first five Gurus, as well as verses by Hindu and Muslim saints. By including the writings of those of other religions, the *Granth* is unique among holy-books. It serves as a perfect example of Sikh tolerance and respect for other religions.

When Guru Gobind Singh compiled the book again, he added the hymns written by the ninth Guru, Guru Tegh Bahadur. In order to distinguish it from his own verses, the *Dasam Granth*, Guru Gobind Singh referred to the original book as the *Adi Granth*, or "First Word". With the authority given to it by Guru Gobind Singh the *Adi Granth* became the basis of the Sikh religion. But it was a lot more than a book of scriptures. It became the representative of the ten Gurus and accordingly is respectfully known as the *Guru Granth Sahib Ji*.

It is written mainly in the Panjabi script, Gurmukhi, although it also includes verses in other languages such as Hindi and Persian. Every copy of the *Granth*, whatever its size, contains 1430 pages and over 3000 hymns, over 2000 having been written by Guru Arjun. Like the other Gurus, he was opposed to ritual and idolatry. He stressed that God was not to be found in outward practices, but in one's own heart:

> Of all Religions this is the best Religion,
> To utter the Holy Name with adoration, and to
> do great deeds:
> Of all rites the holiest rite
> Is to cleanse one's soul in the company of the
> Saints:
> Of all strivings the best striving
> To meditate on the Name and praise it for ever:
> Of all speeches, the ambrosial speech is
> To utter aloud, having hearkened to it, Gods
> glory:
> Of all shrines, the most sacred shrine,
> Nanak, is the heart in which the Lord dwells.

Notice that Guru Arjun uses the name of Nanak. Like the other Gurus, he refers to himself as Nanak. He believed that the spirit of Nanak lived on in him continuing to preach the Word of God. It is that One Spirit living in each of the ten Gurus that Guru Gobind Singh invested into the holy-book.

The *Guru Granth* has become, then, the spiritual guide for the Sikhs throughout their lives.

they never became goals in themselves. Power was always to be used to serve positive ends.

Normally, physical power is seen to conflict with a spiritual life. This is because power – whether it is one person's physical strength or the strength of a ruler's army – is usually used against human interests; to deprive other people of their rights and even of their lives. The Gurus, however, taught that it was even more harmful to human interests to give up power. What was necessary was to use power as a weapon of good and to fight injustice.

## After the Gurus

*The Sikhs against the Mughals*

Before his death, Guru Gobind Singh had appointed Banda Singh as commander of his armies. Banda Singh organized a revolt against the Mughals. In response, they passed an edict that all Sikhs, wherever they were found, were to be killed. This led to a bloody persecution and massacre of Sikhs in an attempt to exterminate them.

Yet their resolve was only strengthened. Thousands of Sikhs fled into the hills and jungles. For a generation they lived virtually on horseback, moving from one place to another to escape detection and certain death. The Panjab was intermittently under the control of these roving Sikh armies until Banda Singh was captured and executed in 1716.

A number of invasions by Afghan armies began to weaken the power of the Mughal rulers. This provided the Sikhs with an opportunity to grow in strength. However they were still subject to widespread persecution, and the area around Lahore was the scene of some of the worst atrocities, including the first "Ghallughara" (holocaust) in June 1746, where 7000 Sikhs were massacred. In Lahore itself is Shahid Ganj ("Place of Martyrs"), in remembrance of the 3000 Sikh prisoners who were publicly executed there.

*The Sikhs against the Afghans*

The Afghan ruler, Abdali, himself proved to be just as ruthless in his clashes with the Sikhs. He sacked

A public execution of a Sikh martyr by the Mughals.

Amritsar a number of times and twice demolished the Harmandir, desecrating the sacred pool with the bodies of dead cows. He is most bitterly remembered for his attack on the village of Kup. It has been estimated that up to 30,000 Sikhs – mainly children, women and old men – were slaughtered on that day. 5 February, 1762, is remembered today as the "Vada Ghallughara" (the great holocaust).

Despite this continuing persecution the Sikhs were able to organize and mobilize an efficient army. In 1765, they captured Lahore and soon extended their power to include the whole country between the Jamuna and the Indus rivers.

*The Sikh Raj*

A national council comprising 12 *misls* (confederacies) was set up and met once a year at Amritsar to settle disputes and discuss matters of national interest. A leader of one of those *misls* was Ranjit Singh. In 1799, at the age of 19, he took overall power and established himself as Maharajah. He made his capital at Lahore, which became the political centre of the Sikh Raj for the next 50 years.

As a ruler he maintained the Sikh ideal of tolerance and allowed complete religious freedom. In fact, many of his chief ministers were Muslims, and the chamberlain of the palace was a Hindu. He made it clear to the people that he was not forming a Sikh kingdom, but a Panjabi state in which Muslims, Hindus and Sikhs would be equal under the law. He also had Europeans and Americans in his service, mainly employed in training his troops.

Although the state was frequently at war and engaged in defence against invasion, it was a time of domestic peace and prosperity. Many *gurdwaras* (places of worship) were built and shrines were restored, including the Harmandir which was rebuilt in marble and covered with gold leaf. Thereafter it became popularly known as the "Golden Temple".

The Golden Temple, the most sacred of Sikh shrines.

In 1839, Maharajah Ranjit Singh died of paralysis, and the Panjab mourned one of its greatest rulers. Under his rule the dream of the Khalsa had come true. They had vanquished their oppressors, and had established their own country. However it was not a situation which would last long.

*The Sikhs against the British*

By this time, the British East India Company had gained a hold over most of India. On the pretext of opening up trade it gave the British government the opportunity to seize political and military power. The British, fearful of the expanding power of the Sikhs, felt it necessary to place a check on them. With the death of the Maharajah the Panjab was divided by a chaotic scramble for power; the British saw their chance and began to move their troops to the Panjabi border. In December 1845, the British Governor General of India issued a declaration of war, in effect stating that the Panjab was to be confiscated and annexed to the British territories.

For over a year, the Sikhs engaged the British in battles, known as the First Anglo-Sikh War. Even the British officers praised the valiance of the Sikhs. However they were finally defeated by traitors in their own camp. Generals Lal Singh and Tej Singh virtually led their own armies to slaughter in exchange for favours from the British. Had it not been for their acts, the British army would have faced a crushing defeat and the whole history of India would have been rewritten. But, as it turned out, the victorious British entered the Sikh capital, Lahore, in February 1846, and the following year a British officer was appointed by the Governor General to be permanently stationed there. Tej Singh was rewarded for his traitorous collaboration with the honorary title of "Raja" (King). Although local dignitaries and chiefs still maintained their land and their titles, they were basically puppets, and ultimate control lay with the British.

Even this rule by proxy, however, did not last. There were a number of small rebellions which, by 1848, escalated into a full-scale war of independence. The British forces were much larger and much better equipped and, in March 1849, after a series of bloody battles costly to both sides, a victory proclamation was made by the British declaring that the Sikh kingdom was at an end. In Lahore, the Sikh flag was lowered and replaced by the Union Jack.

## Under British Rule

*Divide and rule*

It was a rule unlike that of any other invader. The Panjabis had always been used to rulers controlling the country by force and tyranny. They were enemies they knew how to fight. But the British were different. They had won on the battlefield, it was true, but now roads were built, agricultural methods were improved; the Panjab, in general, began to prosper. The people were placated and most began to accept being governed by the British.

On the surface it appeared to be a time of peace and growth. But one group of people can never be governed by another. To keep their self-respect, and to be able to govern their own lives, sooner or later they will rebel. So it was with the Sikhs. The problem facing the Sikhs now was their own disunity.

The strength of the Khalsa had been broken – at least temporarily – and many Sikhs were reverting to Hindu traditions. The caste system which had been so strongly opposed by the Gurus, was now becoming stronger.

During the lives of the Gurus, the Sikhs had been united in their opposition to injustice and tyranny. Since those times, however, they have always been divided by caste, class, politics, and even different religious beliefs. When the British came to power, they kept control mainly by encouraging these divisions and creating new ones; not only within the Sikhs themselves, but also between Sikhs, Hindus and Muslims. The reasoning was simple – if people were divided between themselves, then they could never organize opposition to an outside enemy.

This method was employed throughout the country. So, despite their small numbers, the British were able to control the vastness of India in a way that no conqueror had achieved before. A prime example of this "divide and rule" was displayed during the events of 1857. These are generally known as the "Indian Mutiny", although it is more rightfully seen as the First War of Independence.

*Allegiance to the British*

At the time, there were a number of Indian regiments in the British army. Sikhs, particularly from the Jat and Khatri castes, had been encouraged to enlist. They were renowned for their fighting spirit, and the

British preferred to have them fighting for rather than against them. At the same time, "Untouchables" and low castes were dismissed or excluded from military service. In effect, a "middle-class" was produced which would fight for British interests in return for privileges of status and security.

The grievances which led up to the war in 1857 had been building up for some time. Both Hindus and Muslims, particularly in the army, felt that the British were destroying their religions and their cultures. Although they joined together to fight the British, the Muslims and Hindus each wanted to restore their own rulers. The Sikhs wanted neither. Nor did they share the same grievances. The Sikh soldiers had been allowed to wear the "Five Ks". They were even encouraged to follow the practices of the Khalsa, although, at the same time, being deprived of any real power. Moreover, the Panjab was prospering – it had been a good harvest – and the Sikhs were content.

So, when Hindu and Muslim soldiers began to rebel, the Sikh soldiers, with few exceptions, stayed loyal to the British. They even helped to put down some of the uprisings. Having proved their allegiance during the war, the Sikhs began to form a much larger proportion of the British army. When World War I broke out in 1914 Sikh recruitment was increased and, by the end of the war in 1918, Sikh soldiers numbered over 100,000.

*Towards Independence*

Events in the Panjab, however, gradually began to erode this support for the British Empire, and Sikhs, Hindus and Muslims became united over one aim: to evict the British. Tensions and grievances reached a crisis point and finally erupted in 1919. It was a dark year for the Panjab, but one which was to lead, inevitably, towards the path of Indian Independence.

In Amritsar, Sikhs were gathering to celebrate Baisakhi, the anniversary of the birth of the Khalsa. After praying at the Golden Temple, many collected together at nearby Jallianwala Bagh. They sat and chatted, waiting for the heat of the day to cool down so they could return to their villages.

Unknown to them, the British general R.E.H. Dyer, because of riots the previous day, had declared a state of emergency, and had banned all meetings. As soon as he heard of the gathering at the Jallianwala gardens he assembled his troops and sealed off the only entrance. Without warning, he ordered his men to fire upon the unarmed crowd of men, women, and children: 379 were killed and over 2000 wounded.

The cries of those people still echo in the hearts of Sikhs today. One man is remembered for his attempt to avenge those deaths. In London, March 1940, Udham Singh assassinated Sir Michael O'Dwyer, who, as lieutenant governor of the Panjab, had supported the murderous action of General Dyer. Udham Singh was himself convicted of murder and hanged in London two months later, in June 1940. He had been an active trade-union member in England and in 1938 had founded the first Indian Workers' Association (IWA). To commemorate him, IWAs have since been formed throughout the country.

The massacre at Jallianwala Bagh was followed by a period of greater militancy. In 1920, the Sikhs set up the Central Gurdwara Management Committee, or SGPC (from the initials of its Panjabi name, Shiromani Gurdwārā Prabandhak Committee), to gain control over the *gurdwaras*. As members of the Khalsa had suffered persecution during the previous 200 years, control over the *gurdwaras* had passed into the hands of *mahants* (priestly custodians). The *mahants* generally did not follow the Khalsa discipline and were much closer to Hindu traditions. Even in the Golden Temple Hindu idols were displayed, in direct contradiction to the teachings of the Gurus. As one present-day Sikh put it: "We must be the only people whose places of worship were run by members of another religion!"

To recover their shrines the SGPC formed Sikh volunteers into *jathas* (action-squads). These were then grouped into an organization called the Akali Dal ("Army of Immortals"). Mass campaigns were launched against the *mahants* who were supported by the government. After many bitter confrontations, in which 400 Akalis were killed and 2000 wounded, the Akalis were finally successful. The government gave in to the Akalis' demands and control of the *gurdwaras* was given to the SGPC. Since then, the Akali Dal has always played a major part in Sikh affairs.

Unlike the Akali Dal, who were pledged to non-violence, a number of other groups were formed, convinced that only armed struggle would drive out the British. The largest of these were the Ghadrites

("Revolutionaries") and the Babbar Akalis ("Immortal Lions"). But both were ruthlessly destroyed by the British and their leaders either executed or imprisoned.

Despite the setbacks, the fight for independence had begun. Everywhere, the movement took the form of both armed struggle and passive resistance. Although the Hindu Mohandas Gandhi is usually credited with the eventual victory, a large part of the struggle was waged by the Sikhs, which Gandhi himself acknowledged. When the SGPC won possession of the *gurdwaras*, Gandhi sent them a telegram saying, "Congratulations. First decisive victory for Independence."

*Partition*

When India did achieve Independence, it also had to pay a terrible price. One of the conditions of Independence was that India was to be partitioned into two seperate nation states. The Muslims were agitating to have their own country of Pakistan carved out of the northern Indian states, including the Panjab.

To the Panjabis it spelt nothing less than disaster. The Panjab was to be split into two: 62 per cent of the land, and 55 per cent of the population was to be absorbed into the new Pakistan. This included the richest land, half of the Sikh population, and over 150 historical shrines, including the birthplace of Guru Nanak.

Nothing on paper could describe the total chaos and sheer scale of destruction which took place during this time. Rival gangs of Muslims and Sikhs destroyed whole villages, slaughtering entire populations.

By the winter of 1946-7 there was a mammoth two-way traffic of refugees; Hindus and Sikhs moving from Pakistan into India, and Muslims trekking from India into their new homeland of Pakistan. These human columns were continually attacked by opposing bands resulting in a bloodbath of Hindus, Sikhs and Muslims alike. Apart from the destruction of property, the cost of partition numbered at least half a million lives.

The Sikh refugees left behind vast areas of rich, arable land in Pakistan. Arriving in India, they were given in compensation much smaller areas of less fertile ground. Bringing with them only what they could carry, they had to start all over again.

Of our three families, the only one that was directly affected by the division of the Panjab was the Ratra family. Dr Ratra, who was only four at the time, recalls a vague memory. As a small child he had no understanding of what was happening. All he remembers was chaos: "There were people everywhere. The trains, the stations – everywhere was packed with people." His family was among that fleeing crowd. They abandoned their home in the new Pakistan and travelled to Muzaffanagar, near Delhi. Here his father, who had been a medical officer in the army, decided to settle and open up his own surgery.

Most of the Sikhs, however, decided to settle near Jullunder in East Panjab. But because there was less land to farm, so there was less work. The young men, with no work, began to seek their livelihoods elsewhere. During World War II, many Sikh men had fought in the British army, and now they also began to leave the Panjab to return to where they had been stationed. Looking for work some went back to Singapore and the Philippines. Many went to Canada. Some came to England.

# 2

# The First Sikhs in Britain

Although the majority of Sikhs in this country have arrived here since the 1950s and 1960s, there has been a small number of Sikhs here since the beginning of this century. As early as 1911, a small *gurdwara* was opened in Putney, in London.

Most of the Sikhs were Ramgarhias (from the craftsman caste), or from the small Bhatra caste, who traditionally were hawkers and peddlars. Strictly speaking, the Sikhs do not believe in the caste system, yet these distinctions still continue – even to the present day.

After World War II there was a tremendous boom in industry and new workers were required to help rebuild the British economy. The work available to the new arrivials – nearly all men – was mainly unskilled factory work.

Very few Sikhs had actually come to settle. The majority intended simply to earn enough money to return to the Panjab and buy some land. England, however, did not live up to their dreams of a land paved with gold. It was not so easy to earn a lot of money in a relatively short space of time. They had their own living expenses to pay and, after sending a little of each wage packet back to their families, there was very little to save.

Another major problem was accommodation. Many hostels and boarding houses refused to let rooms to "coloured people". The rooms that were available were highly priced and in extremely poor condition. Rooms were turned into dormitories with rows of beds. Even the beds were not private. They were used on a shift basis – nightworkers sleeping during the day, and dayworkers using the same beds in the night.

To help them cope with this depressing lifestyle,

Britain was a lonely place for those Sikh men who arrived without their families, and for many the separation would last for years. (This photograph, together with those on pages 35, 38 and 39, are taken from a mural painted by Keith Piper and Chila Kumari Burman).

the Sikh men turned back to their own traditions of self-help and mutual support. They began to pool their resources and so were able to buy houses together. This at least lifted the pressure and exploitation of rent payment. In most cases, however, they could only afford the cheapest houses in the most deprived areas. Yet having a place of their own was of tremendous importance to the Sikhs. It gave a sense of stability and also a measure of independence and self-sufficiency. Even today, Sikhs prefer not to be dependent on a landlord, or even an employer. It is very much a Sikh ideal to have one's own home and to be running one's own business.

In their search for jobs, Sikh men often found that they faced discrimination, not only because they were Asian but also because they were Sikh. Many found that wearing a turban made it much harder to secure a job. A typical experience was that of a man applying for a job one day wearing a turban and beard, only to be refused. The next day he might turn up for the same job clean-shaven and with his hair cut, and be accepted. The word soon got round. Many Sikhs cut their hair and shaved their beards.

To do this was a mark of shame as it contravened the instructions of Guru Gobind Singh to the Khalsa. But because of the pressure to find work and earn money, more and more men began to cut their hair. Almost as a compensation, however, many Sikhs, having undergone this outward change, reasserted their faith and culture in other – perhaps more significant – ways. They became much more active in their *gurdwaras* and in their communities.

But still there were those who insisted on wearing the turban. They felt it to be a vitally important part of their faith and identity. Without it, standards would decline, and it would lead to the disintegration of the Khalsa and of the Sikh communities. It was against this latter background that a dispute arose over the right of Sikh bus conductors to wear turbans instead of caps.

The dispute began in 1959 around a Mr G.S.S. Sagar, who was refused a job on the grounds that his turban "did not conform to existing conditions of service". It was a battle which was to rage for seven

Another example of a case where Sikhs have fought to maintain their right to wear the turban.

## Motor-Cycle Crash Helmets (Religious Exemption) Act, 1976

**1976 CHAPTER 62**

An Act to exempt turban-wearing followers of the Sikh religion from the requirement to wear a crash-helmet when riding a motor-cycle. (15th November 1976)

BE IT ENACTED by the Queen's most Excellent Majesty, by and with the advice and consent of the Lords Spiritual and Temporal, and Commons, in this present Parliament assembled, and by the authority of the same, as follows:–

1. In section 32 of the Road Traffic Act 1972 there shall be inserted after subsection (2) the following new subsection:

"(2A) A requirement imposed by regulations under this section (whenever made) shall not apply to any follower of the Sikh religion while he is wearing a turban."

2. This Act may be cited as the Motor-Cycle Crash-Helmets (Religious Exemption) Act 1976.

long years, involving not only the Sikh communities but also local councils and government ministries. Mr Sagar pointed out that during the two World Wars 82,000 turbanned Sikhs had fought and died for Britain. If it was all right to die for Britain wearing turbans, why could they not work in their turbans? He also pointed out that it was a religious requirement to wear a turban; and to be refused employment was to be discriminated against on religious grounds.

Mr Sagar appeared to have the support of the national press as well as of public opinion. The ban had aroused massive publicity in India and was beginning to affect Anglo-Indian relations. After this international publicity, the Transport Committee finally voted in favour of allowing the turban. The irony of the situation was that, by this time, Mr Sagar had passed the maximum age to be a busman. As he said, however, the issue being fought for, was the right of all Sikhs to follow their religion as they themselves chose.

This victory was followed two years later by another, similar dispute in Wolverhampton, in which a Sikh busman was banned from wearing a turban. Again this was won, but only after a group of Sikhs threatened to commit suicide by fire unless the ban was lifted. The consequences of such a threat being carried out would have been disastrous for the British government. Sikhs all around the world were watching the situation with keen interest – and mounting anger. Again, under international pressure, the Transport Committee agreed to observe the Sikh right to wear a turban.

But these were not isolated incidents. During that time and since then to the present day, Sikhs have had to fight continuously to preserve their rights. Perhaps the events mentioned here demonstrate most clearly the Sikh determination and ability to organize in the face of discrimination or persecution. The methods which they used were almost traditionally Sikh in that they had been well tried and tested during campaigns in the Panjab.

3

# Three Families

So far we have looked at a general or collective history of the Sikhs. Let us turn now to our three families and their personal stories.

## The Singh Family

Arriving in 1963, Dyal Singh was the first member of the three families to come to Britain. He was trained as an engineer and, therefore, found it relatively easy to find a job. Like many Sikh men arriving in England, he cut his hair and stopped wearing a turban. He explains why: "For a lot of Sikhs, it was difficult to get a job wearing a turban. For me, there was no problem about a job, because, at that time, they needed engineers. I was able to get a job and still wear a turban. But when I first came I was alone. I was the only Sikh. You just feel watched all the time, you feel vulnerable." It was this pressure to be less noticeable that made him stop wearing a turban.

At first he rented a room in Oxford. Then, when his wife and two sons came to join him, they moved to a flat in Reading. After one and a half years in England, Dyal had saved enough to buy a small house. Surjit Kaur, Dyal's wife, remembers those early days. "It was lonely at first, and I missed my family and parents. There were not many Indian people here then. But we had a few friends and they helped us a lot."

As a result of the cold, damp climate here, and after the birth of her third child, she became very ill. She had to go into hospital leaving her three young children. Back in the Panjab the children would have been looked after by her family, but here there was no one. They had to place the children in foster homes until she was better.

### Sikh Names

A baby's name is usually chosen at the *gurdwara*. The *Guru Granth* is opened at random; the child's name is then chosen beginning with the initial letter of the first word on that page. The sex of the baby is not important as far as naming is concerned, and both boys and girls can receive the same name. Later, they are distinguished by adding "Kaur" for a girl, and "Singh" for a boy. So, for example, the eldest daughter of the Phull family is named Manjit Kaur. If she wishes, she can use the family name, so she becomes Manjit Kaur Phull. Similarly, the son of the Singh family is also Manjit. But he is known as Manjit Singh. The daughter in the family would use the second name Kaur; so, for example, Kulwinder Kaur.

To the British way of doing things, these names are often confusing. Surjit Kaur, the wife of Dyal Singh, is often referrred to as Mrs Singh – though to a Sikh this would not make sense. As Surjit Kaur says, "people in Britain find it strange that a girl or woman does not take her father's or husband's name." This breakdown of family names was originally meant to prevent divisions between family groups, and to prevent women being seen as the property of a particular man or family group.

Sikh children are also given an affectionate nickname. In the case of the Ratra family, Gurpreet and Kanwardeep are called "Monu" and "Bunny" by their parents. These names are usually used throughout childhood, and even when adult, a person may be known mainly by their "pet" name.

Dyal Singh and Surjit Kaur as they are today and just before they arrived in Britain in 1963.

Manjit Singh graduating from university.

As Surjit Kaur's experience shows, it was particularly difficult for Sikh women in this country. Often alone at home looking after small children, and sometimes not speaking English, they remained isolated.

Today, the family is settled in a comfortable house in Reading. Dyal is still working as an engineer and has been involved in constructing a number of buildings in Reading. Surjit used to be a teacher in India but, because of the children, she was not able to work outside the home when she first arrived in England. Now she works in the canteen at Reading University hall of residence.

They now have five children. Manjit, the eldest at 24, now lives in Southall and works at a law centre. He studied law at university and will soon return to finish his solicitor's qualifying exams. This will enable him to achieve his wish and work as a solicitor. Rajinder, 21, has also completed a degree course, in biochemistry, and is about to start a post-graduate course at Reading University.

Surjit Kaur shares her skills with her daughter Rapinder.

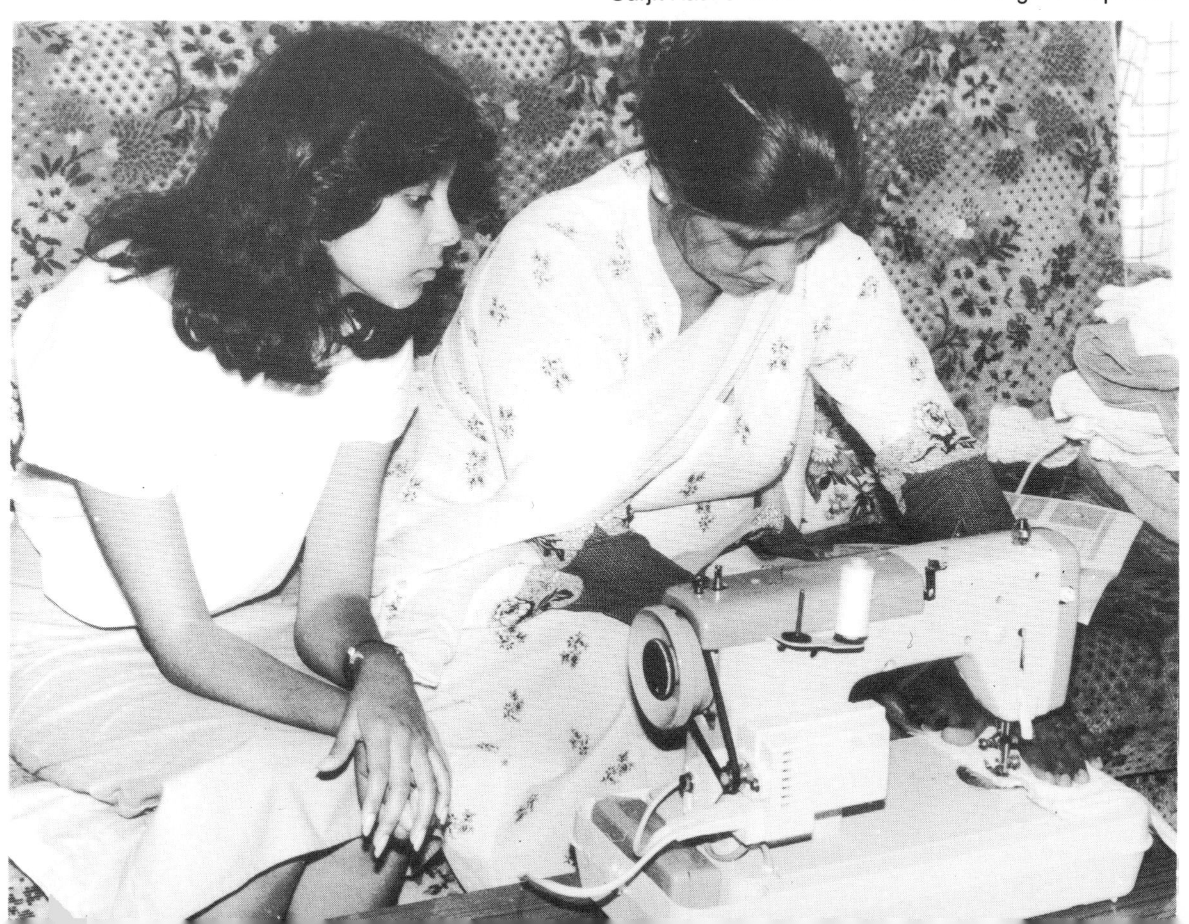

Three generations of the Phull family as they were in Uganda.

Parminder, the eldest daughter, is already married at 19. She works in a bank and is living with her husband in Reading quite close to her parents' house. The two youngest daughters, Kulwinder, 16, and Rapinder, 14, are still at school, Kulwinder has just finished her "O" levels and is hoping to do an accountancy course.

Education is highly valued in the family. Dyal explains his attitude: "We ask our children to try for medicine, law or engineering, but it is up to them. Education is one of the most important things: you never lose it or waste it."

## The Phull Family

Coming from Uganda, the Phull family have had a very different experience. Like all Sikhs, they were originally from the Panjab. But Mr Phull left there in 1950 and travelled to Kenya seeking work. He returned to India two years later to get married, and then went back to Kenya, where he worked for the railways. After the birth of their two eldest children they settled in Uganda. Here, Mr Phull opened a construction business, and the family began to grow and to prosper. Then, in 1972, came the fateful day during the dictatorship of General Idi Amin. An announcement crackled over the radio; "Asians must leave Uganda within 30 days."

The Asians were being depicted as greedy, and the cause of the country's economic troubles. The truth was the exact opposite. Although they formed only 2 per cent of the East African population, the Asians, mainly from the Panjab and Gujarat, had contributed an enormous amount to the development of East Africa. Here again, as in India previously, divisions were created by the ruling powers and exploited within the people. The different African tribes and Africans and Asians were all made to see each other as enemies. Again, this blinded them to the fact that they were all being exploited by a dictator or by a colonial power.

Many Asians, in Kenya for example, took an active part in the struggle for independence from the British. Other Asian businessmen used their wealth to finance newspapers and information sheets which supported independence. For a number of Sikhs, their struggles in East Africa were too similar to the struggles in the Panjab not to be involved.

In Uganda, however, the divisions had been carved too deep and the land was being ruled by fear.

Mr Phull with his son Amarjit serving a regular customer in their East London shop.

The day finally came when the Phulls had to leave. Mrs Phull, with the two youngest children, went to India. Mr Phull, with the four other children, came to England. One day they had a prospering business, a big house, everything they wanted – the next day they arrived in England as refugees without a penny.

They hated England at first; it was very cold, the houses were so small and the people were unfriendly. As Daljit says; "You could live next to a neighbour for years and never get to know them. Back home, friends would just pop round to each others' houses. Here, you feel you can never visit anyone without making a formal arrangement."

For the first five months they stayed with a relative in East London. Then they rented a flat. By this time Mrs Phull and the two boys had come over to join them. In 1974, after two years, Mr Phull bought a house. It was cheap, and needed a lot of work. But with Mr Phull's background in the construction industry he and his wife were able to do the work themselves.

It was a time when they worked very hard, as they both had daytime jobs as well. Mrs Phull was working as a machinist, and Mr Phull was working as a carpenter for the local council. When their day work was over they would come home and begin work on the house. Some of it was heavy building work, and Mrs Phull remembers proudly how she would climb up on to the roof to mend the tiles!

With the success they had with that house, they began to buy old houses, renovate them and sell them again at a profit. Eventually they opened their own business – a shop selling plumbing materials. With his personal experience behind him, Mr Phull was able to supply the right materials as well as give

Mr Phull supervises the youngest son Surjit in the builder's yard of their new shop.

Dr Ratra, on the right, welcomes Mr Kalra, a close family friend who is secretary of the Panjabi Language Development Board.

sound advice to his customers. The business became so successful that they were able to expand. A few hundred yards away, Mr Phull has recently opened another shop, selling building materials. The three younger sons, Amarjit, 21, Paramjit, 18, and Surjit, 16, work in the two shops with their father and help run the deliveries. Daljit, 28, the eldest daughter has just completed an accountancy course and does the accounts for the shops. In this way, the business is very much a family venture. Both Daljit and the eldest son, Narinder, 26, are married and they each run a newsagent's shop. Manjit, 24, the younger daughter, is working for an insurance company.

## The Ratra Family

Our third family, the Ratras, came to Britain in 1973. Surjan Singh Ratra came first and was followed, some months later, by his wife, Parminder Kaur Ratra, and their son, Gurpreet, who was then three. Trained as a doctor of medicine, Surjan Ratra already had a job and accommodation to come to.

Since he has been here, Dr Ratra has furthered his training by studying psychiatry and doing a post-graduate course at the Royal College of Physicians in

Mrs Ratra setting off to drop Kanwardeep at school before going to work.

London. Initially, Mrs Ratra did not do any paid work. In 1975 she gave birth to another boy, Kanwardeep, and was then fully occupied at home looking after her children.

In 1983, when Kanwardeep was eight, she began working with the Manpower Services Commission as a link worker.

Based at a hospital, she is the "link" between the medical staff and the patients. It is often the case that Asian women, in particular, get inadequate, or even wrong treatment because they are unable to explain their symptoms, or understand the instructions from the medical staff. Sometimes, they are simply too afraid to seek treatment. At other times it is the fault of the medical profession. In one case, pregnant Asian women were routinely made to undergo caesarean operations because it was assumed that they were too small to give a "normal" birth.

Parminder's work, then, involves acting as interpreter as well as comforting and reassuring the patients. Recently, she appeared on the Asian television programme *Eastern Eye*, where she explained her work.

Dr Ratra is a prominent and well-respected member of the Sikh community in Birmingham. He is from an affluent family in India and feels that the cultural richness of Indian life has too often been neglected. He cites the example of his marriage which was a very lavish occasion attended by over 500 guests. He feels that it is misleading always to focus on the poverty and problems of India and is concerned that the positive side should also be seen.

Here in Birmingham, the family live in a very comfortable house and are able to enjoy the fruits of life. Yet, at the same time, they have not strayed from their Sikh traditions; they follow their religion very closely. Sikh culture emphasizes hard work and encourages material success. At the same time, it stresses that wealth must be gained by honest means; also, it must not be used for selfish purposes but is to be shared.

Kanwardeep and Gurpreet playing at home on a Saturday afternoon.

Dr Ratra being escorted by his father to his wedding in the Panjab.

4

# SOUTHALL: A Community Comes to Life

Walking down the main streets of Southall one is assailed by a kaleidoscope of sights, smells and sounds. The spicy and fragrant aromas of curries waft out from restaurants; their windows tempting passers-by with mouth-watering displays of Indian sweets. Sari shops are ablaze with colours and patterns. Inside, sales-staff are unwinding roll after roll of shimmering materials for prospective customers. From cassette and video shops, the melodies of Indian music dance out into the streets. Green-groceries overflow on to the pavements with an abundance of fruits and vegetables imported from all over the world. Apart from the shops and restaurants there is a whole range of businesses which serve the community; from Indian marriage bureaux to advice centres to Indian banks. This is Southall.

For Indian people, particularly Panjabis, Southall is a reminder of "home", and a place where they can live according to their own cultures. For Europeans, it is a glimpse of what they imagine India must be like. But behind its "exotic" image lies a very turbulent history, and indeed, a very tense present. The streets may seem lively and colourful, but that is only possible because of the struggles which have taken place to defend and protect those streets.

Let us now look behind the scenes at just how the Sikh community formed and developed.

Situated at the western edge of London, near Heathrow Airport, Southall at first sight appears to be a typical small industrial town. It was, in fact, its industries which first attracted migrant workers, and led to the settling of immigrant communities. Today, Southall has a high percentage of Panjabis, and a majority of these are Sikhs.

## The Sikh Community

In looking at Southall, we gain an impression of Sikh communities throughout Britain, whether it is in Birmingham, Bradford, Leeds, or Glasgow. How the community has developed, and many of the issues that have been a part of its development, have been repeated all over the country. Southall is the story of a Sikh community which has fought to survive. As such, it gives us an understanding of what it means, not only to be a Sikh, but also what it means to be a Black person in this country.

When we talk of a community it is not to imply a group of people living happily together without any conflict. Within the Sikhs in Southall, for example, there are enormous divisions and tensions between the wealthy and the less well-off, between young and old, female and male, between one caste and another, and between different political views. But what makes it into a community is the sharing of a common history and identity. Added to this is the possibility of people working together and supporting each other. In the face of an outside threat, the people of Southall have demonstrated that they are a community.

## Employment in Southall

During the 1950s Southall companies actively sought Asian workers, both to fill the expanding labour demand and to replace the white workers who had moved on from cleaning and factory work to less dirty, better paid jobs. Initially, most of these Asian workers commuted to Southall from as far afield as Aldgate in East London. A few companies – Woolf's rubber factory for example – recruited

The streets of Southall. (*Chaat* is a kind of Indian snack.)

Many Indian families from all over London and beyond often travel to Southall to shop because of the quality, variety and value of goods. Here Mrs Phull and her eldest daughter, Daljit, select their week's groceries.

labour directly from the Panjab. For employers, it was a source of cheap and willing labour.

The general pattern was that Sikh men would arrive in this country first, secure accommodation and employment, and then a few years later send for their families. Slowly they began to form their own informal support and friendship networks. Eventually these led to the first community organizations being set up. By 1957, the Indo-Pakistan Cultural Society and the more radical Indian Workers Association (IWA) had already been formed. A large part of the function of these organizations was educational work in the community. They ran classes, especially in English. Each week they would also show Indian films. These both entertained the new community and helped to lift some of the feeling of homesickness.

In 1959, Southall's first *gurdwara* was set up. Together with the IWA, the *gurdwara* played a crucial role in the growth and welfare of the Sikh community. New arrivals to the country – or just new to Southall – would go to the *gurdwara* where they would receive food, shelter and advice.

In the late 1950s and early 1960s a number of large factories in Southall employed a high percentage of Asian workers. At Woolf's 90 per cent of the unskilled workforce was Sikh. In 1965, after management had unfairly sacked ten workers, the rest of the workforce came out on strike. It was one of the first and – lasting seven weeks – longest strikes by Black workers. Although the strikers did not win their demands, important lessons were learnt. Not only were they resisting the management but they were also opposed by their own union, who refused to support them. The support they received, which helped to maintain the strike, came from the Sikh community itself. The IWA allowed strikers to use their premises, and food and money were collected in the community. Shopkeepers extended credit; landlords agreed to delay rent payments. The Sikhs were continuing their tradition of self-support and independence. The fact that it was in a new country made no difference.

It was not only the men who faced and fought injustice in the labour force. From the early 1960s onwards, when the women came to join their husbands in England, they found that a single wage was not enough to support a whole family. The women were forced to seek paid work outside the home. From Asian-owned shops and restaurants, they began to seek work in factories, hospitals and service industries. Often they spoke little English and were unfamiliar with the politics of the work situation. As a result they were given the least skilled, worst paid jobs and were in no position to organize the improvement of conditions or pay.

Heathrow Airport is the largest employer of Southall's Asian women, who work mainly in the cleaning and catering areas. As the work is on a shift basis, the women sometimes have to be up by 4 a.m. to get to work, or arrive home very late at night. Conditions are hard and racial discrimination rife. In 1975, 450 Asian workers walked out. Although they stayed out on strike for only one week, it was long enough to win them a number of concessions.

There have been a number of other struggles by Sikh men and women – not all involving strikes. These have included successful demands for better pay, improved working conditions, child-care provision, and so on.

## Housing Problems

As families began to arrive in Britain, this led to another problem – housing. As industry expanded, so more people began to move into Southall. The housing was old and there was not enough of it. As better, more expensive houses were built in the "green areas" around Southall, so some of the better-off white owners could afford to sell their own houses in the town centre and move out. This began to create a "ghetto", where the old houses in the centre, often without proper sanitation, became the only housing available to the newly arrived immigrant families. Moving into conditions which were already overcrowded and inadequate, the immigrant population came to be blamed for the problems which were there already. The obvious and practical solution was to build more housing. Yet government, on a local and national level, was not prepared to do this. Instead, it began to prosecute families for overcrowding. Thrown out of what little accommodation they had, people were forced on to the streets.

## Education

As Sikhs began to settle here, the education of their children became one of their main priorities. Education was seen as a means of improving their children's chances in British society. Yet, even here, the children were targets of discrimination, not just

Employment was often beset with problems so the community pulled together to improve wages and working conditions.

R. WOOLFS RUBBER CO.
NESTLE
ROCKWAR GLASS
1951
IWA
LABOUR FORCE ON STRIKE!
AGAINST RACIST DISMISSALS AT WOOLFS
MUST WE WORK 75 HOURS a WEEK FOR A LIVING WAGE?
INDIAN WORKERS ASSOCIATION

A police officer keeps watch outside the Singh Sabha *gurdwara* in Southall.

on an individual basis, but also by government policies. Most Sikh children attended certain schools in the centre of Southall. In one school, for example, 58 per cent of the pupils were from immigrant (mainly Sikh) families. In 1963, the government decided to impose a maximum limit of 33 per cent of "immigrant children" at any one school. This quota was adopted along lines purely of colour, and not on educational ability. Once a school reached the 33 per cent limit, any extra immigrant pupils were "bussed" out to schools in surrounding areas. This increased their isolation: they were not able to continue friendships outside school-hours because of the geographical distance between friends. By 1973 2500 children were being "bussed". They were automatically placed in "reception" classes, and to a large extent were segregated from the main school. It was often assumed that these pupils were incapable of learning and so in many cases they were neglected and received inadequate or inferior teaching. They also came under physical attack from other pupils. Attacks reached such proportions that in some cases teachers used to guard Asian children waiting for buses.

The Asian children, however, had their own solutions. Older Asian pupils from other schools would escort the younger children to and from school, and would be there at lunchtime and breaks to protect them.

## Relations with the Police

Slowly the community's faith in the British institutions was being undermined, but this was, in turn, bringing about a split between Sikh youth and their elders. The older generation placed their faith in negotiations and petitions; most of them hoped to sway the authorities by gentle means. For the more volatile young Sikhs, these methods had been tried and had failed. They demanded action. The spur which led them to this position was the death of one of their own. In June 1976, Gurdip Singh Chaggar was stabbed to death outside the Dominion Cinema in Southall. The next morning small groups of angry Asian youths were beginning to gather and there were outbreaks of violence. The police were called and began indiscriminately to stop and search Asian youths. This added to the general feeling that the police were more interested in policing the Asian community than in catching Chaggar's murderers. The IWA called a meeting to condemn the murder and the subsequent police action, but went no further. Disenchanted by the IWA's lack of action, the youth met separately and decided to organize self-defence units. This meeting laid the foundation for the forming of Southall Youth Movement (SYM).

In 1979, the community was again faced with another threat. On 23 April, the National Front planned to hold a meeting at Southall Town Hall. They had no support in the area; they had not even had a candidate there for nearly ten years. It was a calculated attempt to insult and provoke the Black

A cordon of police carrying riot shields holds back demonstrators as they voice their anger at the National Front meeting on 23 April, 1979.

communities. In this, they succeeded. It also had the effect of shattering the last remnants of faith that some sections of the community had in the police and in local and national government. Despite persistent appeals from community leaders, the local council refused to ban the meeting. To the community this was virtually the same as the council supporting the National Front. Plans were prepared for a peaceful protest to take place on the day. When the day arrived nearly 3000 police – with dogs, horses, and riot equipment – sealed off the town centre. Nearly 350 demonstrators were arrested and charged, many were injured. One was killed. Blair Peach received a fatal blow to the head from a police truncheon. The National Front meeting went ahead as planned. As far as the community was concerned the police were protecting the fascists. In order to do that they were even prepared to kill.

Panjabi newspapers compared the day to the massacre of 1919 at Jallianwala Bagh in the Panjab. The feeling had grown that, despite the British Empire having appeared to have ended, Southall was still a colony and its inhabitants still colonized. The colonizing force this time was not the British army but the British police. Eye-witnesses were reported in the *Daily Telegraph* (24 April) to have seen ". . . several dozen crying, screaming, coloured demonstrators being dragged . . . to the police station and waiting coaches. Nearly every demonstrator we saw had blood flowing from some sort of injury; some were doubled up in pain."

Racist attacks continued in the area. In July 1981, during what was termed as the "Southall riots" three coachloads of "skinheads" travelled into Southall to attend a concert at the notorious Hambrough Tavern. On their way to the pub they terrorized

TUC
IWA
SOUTHALL
Hambrough Tavern
THALL YOUTH MOVEMENT TO
REMEMBERS
BLAIR PEACH
AND
GURDIP SINGH CHAGGAR
NEVER AGAIN!
STOP THE NAZIS THE NF!
JULY 1981
ASIAN YOUTH
RUN THE NAZIS
OUT OF SOUTHALL

shopkeepers and shoppers, smashing windows and shouting abuse at passers-by. Word quickly got round, and soon several hundred local youths, mainly Asian, both men and women, gathered to defend their community. The police arrived, again, it seemed, to protect the aggressors. Pitched battles followed. The Hambrough was burnt down and the "skinheads" retreated. The next day, the young people of Southall declared, "if the police will not protect our community, we have to protect ourselves".

The threat to Southall from outside led to a greater militancy, resulting in a number of groups being formed to defend and strengthen the community.

## Defence Organizations

Far from being beaten, the community began to pull together and became stronger. A number of organizations were formed to fight racism, and also to improve facilities in the area. The community had not only been defended by the men, but also by the women. The stereotype of the passive Asian woman had long come under siege. One of the results of the women's participation was the formation of Southall Black Sisters which began to compaign particularly over issues affecting women, but also to act as a balance to the male-dominated IWA and SYM.

Two legal advice centres were set up to support the rights of members of the community. One of them is the Southall Law Centre where Manjit Singh works. He deals with legal problems, particularly

Manjit Singh at work in the law centre discussing a case with a client.

those regarding employment, and has often taken up cases of racial discrimination and unfair dismissal. The number of cases the centre has to deal with indicates that the problems which Asian workers face today have not diminished since the 1950s when they first began to work in Southall.

Dealing with issues such as police harassment and racist attacks are other groups, such as the Southall Monitoring Group. Again, the fact that there is even the need for such groups shows that these problems, too, continue.

Unlike the events of April 1979, or July 1981, the everyday work of these organizations rarely makes the headlines; but, without them, Southall would be much weaker in its struggle to survive as a community.

STATISTICS, 1st. APRIL, 1984 – 31st. MARCH, 1985

| | No. of CASES | % | No. of ENQ. | % |
|---|---|---|---|---|
| Housing | 160 | 17 | 310 | 7.5 |
| Welfare Rights | 334 | 35 | 2298 | 51 |
| Immigration | 132 | 14 | 1024 | 23 |
| Family + Domestic Violence | 83 | 9 | 144 | 3 |
| Crime | 67 | 7 | 105 | 2 |
| Consumer | 18 | 2 | 109 | 2 |
| Employment | 79 | 8 | 139 | 3 |
| Other | 70 | 8 | 390 | 8.5 |
| | 943 | 100% | 4519 | 100% |

A table of cases and enquiries dealt with by the Southall Law Centre.

## Community Development

Working alongside these "defence organizations" are a number of other groups, which are trying to bring new facilities into Southall and to develop the amenities already there. A number of arts organizations have been formed in the area. Their emphasis is on developing the skills of the young people in Southall and creating art forms which are a combination of traditional cultures and a present-day experience of life in this society. As well as staging art exhibitions and theatre performances, they also organize workshops and classes. These range from drama workshops, to dance, pottery, film, print-making, photography and painting. Because of the high level of youth unemployment in the area, these sorts of activities serve a very important purpose.

Other organizations have turned their energies to providing sports facilities. Some of the most common sports amongst the Sikh community are hockey, badminton, wrestling and *kabbadi*. These sports are particularly popular in India, and Sikhs are internationally renowned for their sporting prowess. *Kabbadi* is almost unknown here apart from amongst Panjabi communities. It is played by two teams, usually of men, on a rectangular court. A player from one team crosses the centre line and tries to touch a player of the other team. If he manages, he

Amarjeet Kaur Gujral, a Sikh artist and poet, with one of her works.

Kabbadi as played here in a village in India (above) is becoming increasingly popular in Britain, as shown by this event organized by the Southall Youth Movement.

then has to run back to his own side without his opponent stopping him. All the while he has to keep saying "Kabbadi, Kabbadi". He only scores a point if he manages to touch an opponent and get back to his own side before running out of breath.

As well as the new arts organizations, there are also the more traditional arts, especially music and dance, which continue to be extremely popular, even among young Sikhs. Of the Panjabi folk music, perhaps the most popular dances are the "Bhangra" and the "Gidha". These are performed by men and

Bhangra, a traditional dance form, still remains popular with the young, as shown by this poster.

Mr Phull and his son Surjit playing the harmonium and *tabla*. Surjit, who was taught by his father, says to be able to play correctly you have to practise for weeks just to learn the basics.

A video shop in Southall catering for the increasing demand.

women respectively. Originally based on harvest rituals, they are now performed at any celebration. The rhythm for the Bhangra is provided by large side drums played with sticks, but in the women's dance – Gidha – the drumming is replaced by clapping. In both dances, a circle is formed with one pair in the centre who lead the dance. One of the pair sings a line to which the others dancing round respond in a chorus. After each verse, a new pair go into the centre. There are traditional lyrics, especially for particular festivals. But the participants are free to make up their own lines, which are often remarks about the audiences or some recent event. You can be sure, whatever the celebration, that the Bhangra is going to be a lively, joyful affair.

The most common percussion instruments, which are also used during *kirtan* (hymn singing) at the *gurdwara*, are the *tabla* (hand/finger drums), and the three types of side-drum, *dholi, dhola,* and *dholak*. Melody is usually provided by a harmonium, as well as the *sarangi* (a stringed instrument like a fiddle). *Bansri* (a flute) and *langoja* (a pair of pipes) are also played.

Another popular source of entertainment is Indian films. There used to be a number of cinemas in Southall showing Indian films. The boom in videos, however, has meant that families now prefer to watch those films in the comfort of their own homes. The cinemas, which were once a popular social point, have closed down and now lie empty.

5

# The *Gurdwara*

When we look at a Sikh community, we find that it revolves around a *gurdwara*. More than being simply a place of worship, the *gurdwara* is vital to maintaining any Sikh community. As we have seen earlier in Southall, the *gurdwara* was often the first place to which visitors would go. Here, they would find food, shelter and advice. *Gurdwaras* are open to everyone, regardless of religion, race or sex.

The functioning of the *gurdwara* is firmly based on the principle of equality. There is no priestly hierarchy; instead a management committee is elected by the community. This carries out the administration and the daily running of the *gurdwara*. Often there is a full-time caretaker who may also be a "Granthi" (one who reads from the Holy Book). Granthi can be male or female, although in practice they are usually male. Again, they will not have any real authority but will be performing a service for the community.

The coming together in communal worship is a vital and necessary part of Sikh life. When the community comes together in the name of the Gurus

Women preparing *roti* which will be served at the *langar*.

then they, like the holy-book, the *Guru Granth*, become a living representation of the ten Gurus. The Sikh community is then referred to as the "Guru Panth".

*Gurdwaras* in Britain may vary enormously depending on the type and size of building available. The Sri Guru Singh Sabha *gurdwara* in Southall, for example, consists of a large hall where the "Sangat" (congregation) meets. Upstairs, although not directly above the hall, are offices where the organization of the *gurdwara* is carried out. Downstairs again, behind the hall is a *langar* ("free kitchen"), where food is prepared for the congregation.

Before entering the *gurdwara*, each person removes his or her shoes and makes sure his or her head is covered. Women usually use a *dupatta* (scarf). Men, if they are not wearing turbans, simply use a piece of cloth or a handkerchief.

The *Guru Granth* is kept in the large hall, resting on cushions on a *diwan* (platform). The *diwan* is more correctly a *takht* (throne). In this way it is given the same respect as if it were a living Guru. A Granthi or a *sewadar* (volunteer) sits constantly in attendance behind the *Guru Granth*, and holds a *chowr* (a whisk, symbolic of a ruler). When the *Guru Granth* is not being read, it is kept closed and covered with *ramala* (silk cloths).

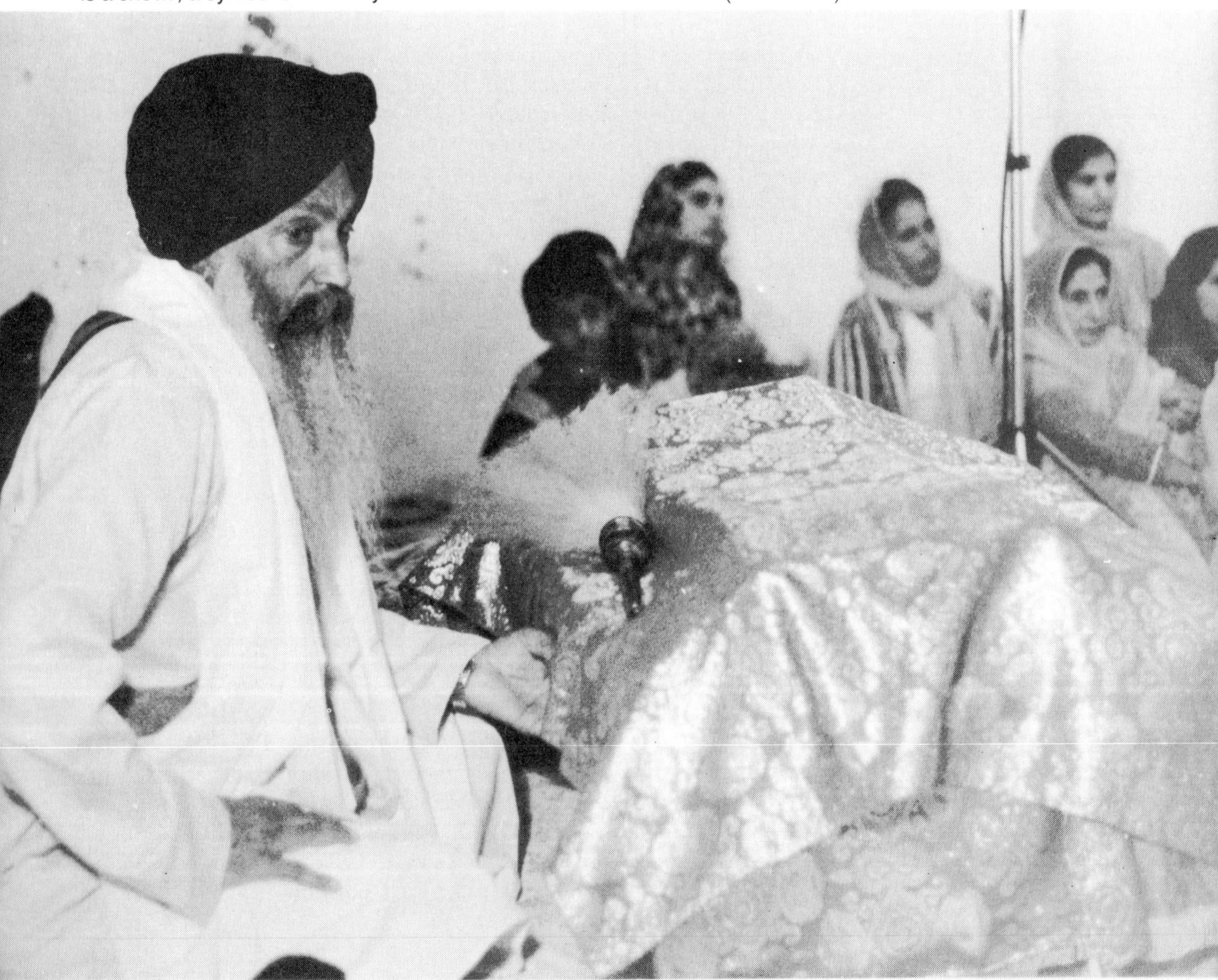

A Granthi attends the covered *Guru Granth*; before him is a *chowr*, a symbol of authority.

As people enter the hall, they approach the *diwan* and bow to the ground in respect. Usually a small offering is made, either of money or food. They then find a place to sit; women on one side, men on the other. Everyone sits cross-legged on the floor, to indicate that there is no hierarchy.

### A Sangat

A Sangat can begin when there are five or more people present. The *Guru Granth* is opened at random and the Granthi recites whatever is on that page beginning at the top left-hand corner. This random choice of reading is called a *wak*.

After the *wak* there is *kirtan* – singing of *shabads* (hymns) from the *Guru Granth*. On special occasions, professional musicians may lead the *kirtan*, but usually it is someone from the Sangat. In between the *kirtan*, there is *ketha* (exposition). This may be an explanation of the passage already read from the *Guru Granth:* it could be a story, a poem, or a speech about a particular event. Again, anyone from the Sangat has the chance to speak if he or she wishes. When the *kirtan* has finished, then business matters, such as the running of the *gurdwara*, and discussions on political issues take place. This could be about local matters or relate to international events. Often, newspaper articles are pinned to the *gurdwara* noticeboard, and these might be discussed inside. These discussions are led by a member of the management committee or by any member of the community.

The Sangat serves a very necessary function in bringing people together to discuss matters affecting their individual lives as well as events affecting them as a people. In this way it develops and coordinates not only Sikh religious thought but also Sikh political opinion.

The Sangat is also very much a family occasion, and the atmosphere is informal and lively. People rarely stay for the whole Sangat, which can last as long as four hours. It is much more likely that people will come for only a short while, meet some friends outside and maybe eat at the *langar*. Young children, who are not expected to pray, are free to run out and play and then return when they feel less restless. Families are able to meet relatives and friends, and, for the women and children, going to the *gurdwara* might be their only social outing. For the children it often means they can meet other young Sikhs in an environment which their parents approve of.

The end of the Sangat is marked by the distribution of Karah Prashad. This is a sweet made from semolina, milk, butter and sugar, and flavoured with cinnamon. Like the food in the *langar*, the sharing of Karah Prashad creates a unity and sense of equality amongst the congregation.

The meals served at the *langar* are always vegetarian, so that everyone is able to eat. The meal is usually quite simple. A typical example would be *dal* (lentils), *sabzi* (vegetables), *dahi* (yoghurt) and *roti* (flat bread).

### Other Functions of the *Gurdwara*

As well as being a place of worship, the *gurdwara* is also a place of religious education. Here children can learn about the Sikh religion and its history. Some *gurdwaras* maintain a library for this purpose. Perhaps one of the most important classes is Panjabi. Although Sikh children may speak Panjabi at home, very few of them will have learnt to read or write it. Until they can, they will not be able to read the *Guru Granth* in its original form. Obviously, Sikh elders worry about this. They fear that with each new generation there will be fewer and fewer Sikhs who can read their own holy-book.

The *gurdwara* is open every day and it is an ideal that it is always a place of shelter. In India, the big *gurdwaras* would maintain a *langar* 24 hours a day to feed a constant stream of pilgrims. In Britain, the smaller *gurdwaras* might have a *langar* only once a week, while the larger ones will try to provide a meal each day. Although the Sikhs do not observe a holy day of the week, Sunday has become the most convenient day when most people are free from work to be able to attend the *gurdwara*. So this is the day which is generally set aside for the large Sangat. However, many Sikhs, especially the older ones, make a point of going to the *gurdwara* every day.

### Festivals and Celebrations

In the Panjab, there are a number of festivals and commemorations throughout the year. Some are small, village celebrations to do with a local shrine of a place where one of the Gurus was present. Others, like Baisakhi in April and Diwali in October, are major gatherings which originally were connected to harvest and seasonal activities.

Some festivals are known as "Gurpurbs". These

੧ੴ ਸ੍ਰੀ ਵਾਹਿਗੁਰੂ ਜੀ ਕੀ ਫਤਿਹ ॥

| | |
|---|---|
| **ਖਾਲਸਾ ਮੇਰੋ ਰੂਪ ਹੈ ਖਾਸ ।** | **Khalsa is my own special form** |
| **ਖਾਲਸੇ ਮਹਿ ਹੌ ਕਰੌ ਨਿਵਾਸ ॥** | **I always manifest in the Khalsa** |
| ਜਾਗਤ ਜੋਤ ਜਪੈ ਨਿਸ ਬਾਸੁਰ, | **And he who repeats the name of the omnipresent day and night** |
| ਏਕ ਬਿਨਾ ਮਨ ਨੈਕ ਨ ਆਨੈ। | **Sets not his thoughts on any other but one almighty.** |
| ਪੂਰਨ ਪ੍ਰੇਮ ਪ੍ਰਤੀਤ ਸਜੈ, ਬ੍ਰਤ | **Who is ever imbued with his presence everywhere.** |
| ਗੋਰ ਮੜ੍ਹੀ ਮਟ ਭੂਲ ਨਾ ਮਾਨੈ । | **And observes (believes) no fast and bows not to the graves.** |
| ਤੀਰਥ, ਦਾਨ, ਦਯਾ, ਤਪ, ਸੰਜਮ, | **Who attaches little value to pilgrimages and austerities.** |
| ਏਕ ਬਿਨਾ ਨਹਿ ਏ ਪਛਾਨੈ । | **And recognises the authority only of one God.** |
| ਪੂਰਨ ਜੋਤਿ ਜਗੈ ਘਟ ਮੈਂ | **In his blessed heart will dwell the perfect Lord.** |
| ਤਬ ਖ਼ਾਲਸਾ ਤਾਹਿ ਨਖਾਲਸ ਜਾਨੈ । | **And only he deserves to be called "Khalsa".** |
| **ਜਬ ਲਗ ਖਾਲਸਾ ਰਹੇ ਨਿਆਰਾ** | **As long as Khalsa remains distinctive** |
| **ਤਬ ਲਗ ਤੇਜ ਦੀਉ ਮੈਂ ਸਾਰਾ।** | **I shall bestow glory on him.** |

▲ The inside page of a Baisakhi greetings card.

Sikh disciples receiving baptism into the Khalsa community. ▼

commemorate the births and deaths of the Gurus and major events in their lives. In Britain the celebrations take place on a much smaller scale. As always, the *gurdwara* is the focus of any activities. During the major festivals, as well as more private functions such as a marriage, there is an "Akand Path". This is a continuous recital of the entire *Guru Granth*. Taking about 36 hours, it is done by relays of Granthis. Usually begun on a Friday evening, it is timed to finish for the Sangat on Sunday morning.

Baisakhi, the first day of Baisakh, the Spring Harvest Festival in the Panjab, is celebrated now also as a commemoration of the founding of the Khalsa by Guru Gobind Singh. This has always been a major gathering for the Sikhs and, because of that, was also a time when bloody battles have been fought. The history of Baisakhi then, has been a mixed one – full of glory, but also of bloodshed and mourning. Today, such a history is imprinted into the hearts and minds of Sikhs; Baisakhi is a time of high emotions.

## The Baptism Ceremony

Baisakhi is also the time when many Sikhs are "baptized" into the Khalsa. For a Sikh it is one of the most important ceremonies in his or her life. The ceremony itself is done as it was first carried out by Guru Gobind Singh.

*Amrit* (nectar) is prepared in an iron bowl, and made from sugar dissolved in water. This is then stirred by five Sikhs (the "Panj Piyare") using a *khanda* (a double-edged sword). A Granthi reads the "Japji" (a hymn by Guru Nanak) while the others squat in the *vir asan* position, or position of the warrior. This is simply a resting position, but in a state of readiness as a warrior should be (the left knee rests on the ground while the right knee is raised ready to leap up). After other poems have been read, those waiting to be "baptized" approach. Each person recites the words "Wahe Guru Ji Ka Khalsa Sri Wahe Guru Ji Ki Fateh" (the Khalsa is of God and the Victory is to God). While doing so, they sip *amrit* from the hands of one of the Panj Piyare. This is repeated five time. *Amrit* is then sprinkled into the eyes and, moving aside the turban or head covering, is then placed on the head of each disciple. After each one has been "baptized", the "Anand" ("Song of Bliss") is sung and prayers are offered.

Those baptized have now been accepted into the community of the Khalsa.

# 6

# Family Life

The home life of Sikhs is usually very different from the lives they lead at school, college or work. Sometimes it can be a positive element but it can also be negative. Home can serve as a sanctuary from the pressures of outside life; it can also act as a prison, restricting the lives of young people especially. Later on, we shall look at some of these conflicts in more detail.

Most Sikh homes act in some way to reinforce Sikh culture. It is in the home that people are free to practise their own traditions. Young Sikhs will generally grow up in a home environment where they are continually reminded of their religious culture and identity. There may be pictures of the

The Singh family relaxes at home. Despite the influences of television and Western music, the traditions of Sikhism still maintain their presence through the portraits of the Gurus.

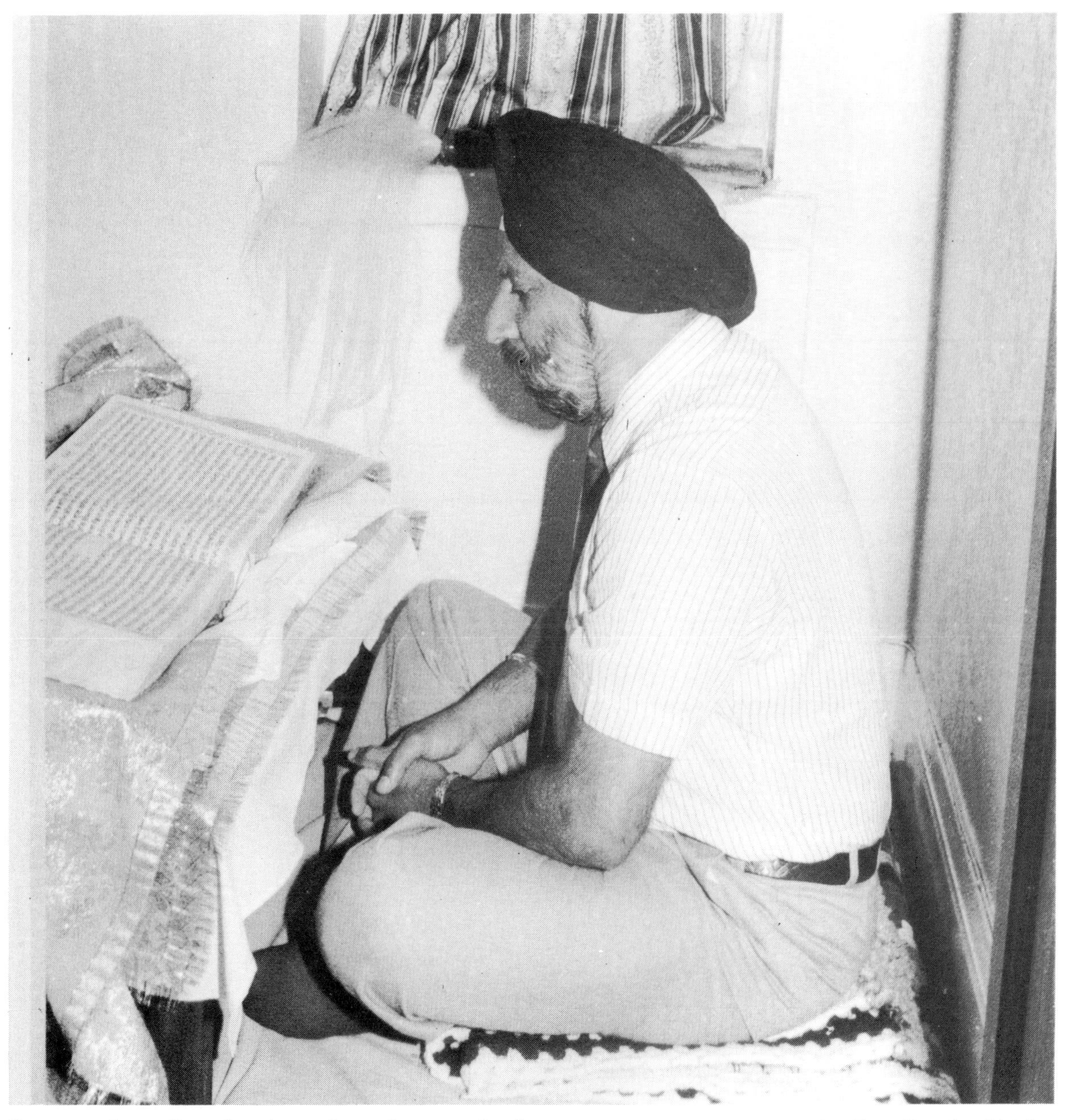

Dr Ratra reading verses from the *Guru Granth*, which is kept in a special prayer room.

Gurus on the walls and perhaps also a photograph of the Golden Temple. Sometimes wall plaques are engraved in Gurmukhi script, and hung on the front door or in the hall.

Some families, like the Ratras, keep a copy of the *Guru Granth* in their homes. Because of the respect shown to it, it is kept in a separate room, which functions as a shrine or a prayer room. Obviously, not many families are able to afford this extra space. Instead, the family might just have small prayerbooks. These contain special prayers for the morning and evening. There might also be included some passages from the *Guru Granth*. Some verses provide instructions for one's daily life. Here is an example written by Guru Ram Das, the Fourth Guru:

Mrs Ratra with her sons, Gurpreet and Kanwardeep, at their school fete.

He who would call himself a Sikh of the True Guru
Should rise early in the morning and contemplate the name.
In the early hours of the morning, he should rise and bathe,
And cleanse his soul in a tank of nectar.
As he repeats the Name the Guru taught him,
He washes away the sins of his soul.
Then at dawn he should sing the hymns of the Guru
Throughout the business of the day,
He should hold in his heart the Name.
He that repeats the Name with every breath
Such a Sikh is indeed dear to the Guru.

Of course, this was written for a very different lifestyle. In Britain's cities very few Sikhs live according to these instructions. Life is much more rushed than it would be in a Panjab village. Here, for those who go out to work, it becomes inconvenient to bathe and pray in the early morning.

Young children are unaffected, anyway. They are not expected to take part in prayers. They may simply be taught to say "Satnam Waheguru" ("The True Name of the Great Guru" – which is a respectful name for God).

The Phull family sitting down together for their evening meal. They eat from *thalis* (stainless steel trays), which have separate sections to hold the different kinds of food.

### Western Influence

Although children may grow up in an atmosphere where they are surrounded by their parents' traditions and religion, often little attempt is made to explain the meaning of things. They are expected to follow the traditions but without understanding the reasons behind them. As they get older, they begin to notice more and more the differences between their own lifestyle and those of their school-friends. In comparison, their own lives might appear to be very restricted and unfair.

This is a problem for the whole family to solve, as it requires a lot of patience and understanding from the parents. Surjan and Parminder Ratra are both aware, through their work, of the pressures and conflicts which their children, Gurpreet and Kanwardeep, are likely to face. They feel that the best way to prepare and deal with this is to have complete honesty within the family, and to discuss any problems which may arise. They would prefer their children to respect and follow the Sikh teachings; at the same time, they are careful not to enforce their views. According to Surjan, "children should have a full idea of their own culture and their own community. From this position they will be able to choose wisely, and not just react blindly against their own traditions."

Unfortunately, what sometimes happens in families is that whenever children start demanding more freedom the parents, in fact, become stricter. They justify this by saying that they are doing it for the children's good and they are trying to maintain their culture.

Some families, especially those from East Africa like the Phulls, are often more tolerant. This is probably because, having moved from India to Africa, they have already broken away from the tighter restrictions which families in the Panjab might experience. Also they would be more confident in a different culture and more able to cope with Western city life.

Mr and Mrs Phull follow their traditions much more closely than their children. Mr Phull goes to the *gurdwara* every evening and takes an active part in its affairs. The children are much more Western in their tastes and attitudes. For example, none of the sons wear turbans, and they have an enormous amount of freedom as to how they lead their lives. The two boys, Amarjit and Paramjit, commonly use the names George and Tony. Yet this movement away from Sikh traditions has not threatened the unity of the family in any way. They would still follow their parents' instructions over important decisions. Their parents probably know this, and at the same time know that their children will never rebel, because they have no need to.

### Attitudes Towards Daughters

In most families, however, parents are much stricter with their daughters than they are with their sons. Daljit remembers when she lived at her parents' home before she was married: "The boys were able to go out whenever they wanted, but for me it was more difficult. My parents wanted to know where I was, who I was with, and what time I would be back."

In some families, apart from school, the girls are not allowed out at all. One younger girl tells of a

Rapinder and Kulwinder help their mother prepare the evening meal at their home in Reading. Rapinder, on the left, is making *rotis* while her mother, on the right, is heating *dal* in the microwave oven.

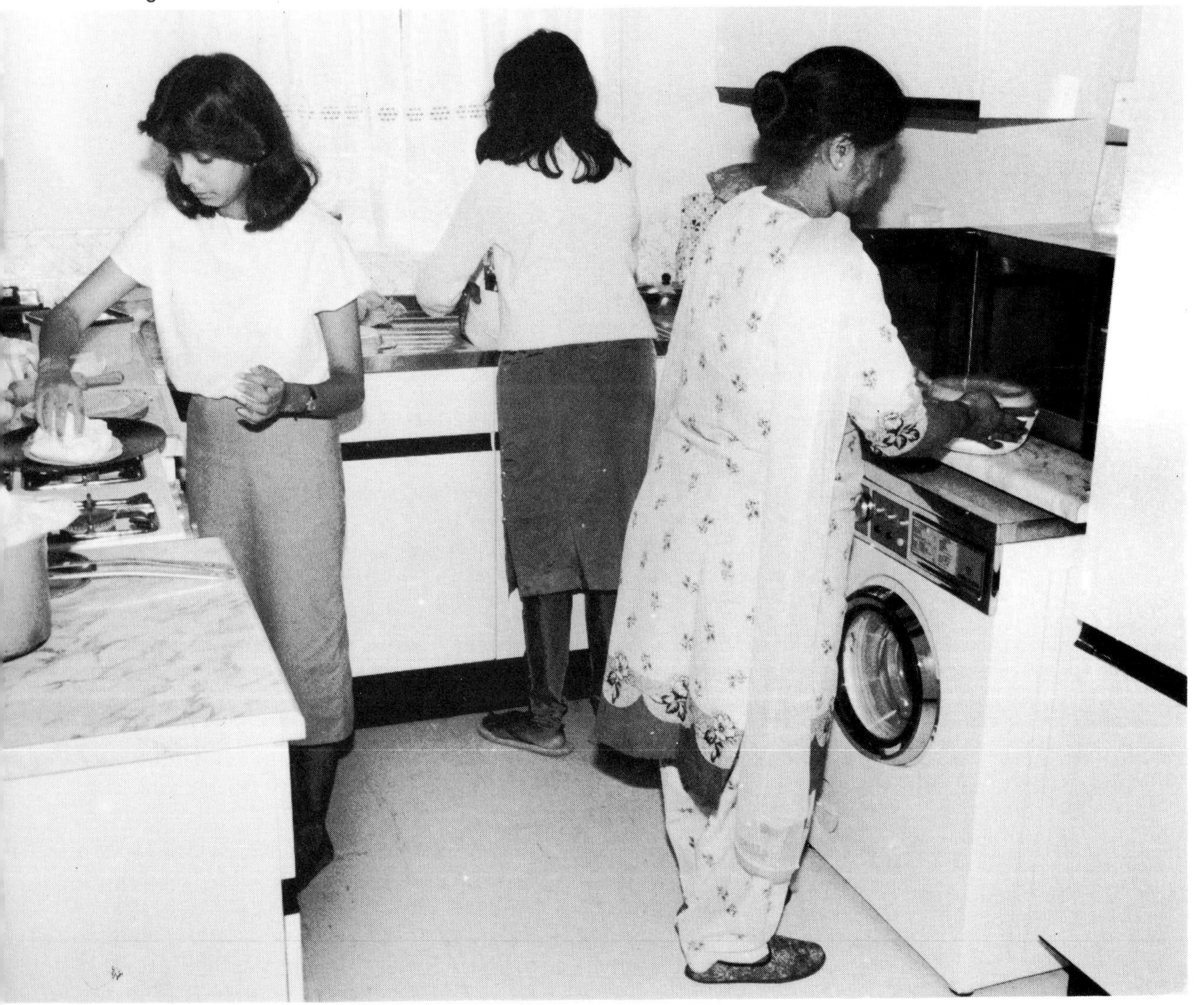

typical situation: "My friends can visit me; but they've stopped asking me out for parties or anything because they know I can't go out."

Girls are taught from a very early age to help in the house, and by the time they reach their teens, are expected to share a large part of the housework. At the same time, they are expected to devote a good deal of time to their studies. As one girl puts it: "It's the same routine nearly every evening – I come home from school and have to do the housework and my homework. Only when all that is finished, then I might be able to watch some television."

Sometimes, though, education for girls is not regarded as an end in itself or as a step towards a career, but as another "attraction" to get her a better marriage partner. Parents also fear, however, that if a girl goes to college or university she will become too influenced by Western society. The chances are higher, then, of her rejecting a marriage which they have arranged for her. The girl herself knows that as long as she is studying then it is unlikely that her parents will try to get her married. One young Sikh woman explains her situation: "Marriage is one thing I worry about. As long as I study it's okay. But when I stop studying I will have to get married. I want to study, and I also want to get married – but not so early." Here she begins to laugh, "So I'll just have to study as long as possible!"

## Arranged Marriages and the Family Unit

Behind the laughter lies a serious worry. Marriage is an issue which every young Sikh woman confronts. We sometimes read sensationalized reports in newspapers about Indian women committing suicide rather than going through an arranged marriage or accounts are given of young women being forced to marry men they have never met.

How does an arranged marriage actually work? Obviously it varies from family to family, some being much stricter than others. But, in general, the word "arrangement" does not mean that the spouse has no choice at all.

The young man or woman is allowed to meet a number of potential partners. These can be proposed by the parents or relatives. One of the most common ways of finding a partner is through a marriage bureau or by placing advertisements in appropriate newspapers. A number of Asian newspapers have matrimonial columns for this purpose.

The process of finding a partner can take anything from a few weeks to several years. Parents, who are trying to find the best choice for their children, are usually quite lenient in this respect. However, as time passes there may be pressure applied, not so much from the parents but more from relatives, who begin to wonder why the son or daughter is still unmarried. Often, it is this kind of pressure from relatives which determines decisions taken within the family. It would be quite unusual to find a man,

Marriage advertisements from an Indian newspaper in Britain.

**Jat Sikh parents require a suitable match for their daughter, born in U.K., 22 years old, 5'3" tall, from a respectable family from District Jalandhar. Parents have settled in U.K. for over 25 years. She is doing B.A. in Business Studies, and is currently in the 3rd year of the 4 years course. She also holds a Scottish National Certificate in Business Studies. Boy should be betwen 23-28 years of age.**

Parents in Canada seek qualified, professional, healthy, handsom, clean shaven, Jat Sikh match (non smoker) for their qualified professional daughter, 5-3', 23 years old, pretty, slim, healthy, B.Business Adm. Canadian University employed as an Accountant.

**Wanted a suitable match for a Ramgarhia Sikh male of age 26 years, 5'10" tall, he holds the M.Sc.degree and is a Lecturer in Physics. He has been in the U.K. for over 23 years and is a householder. The girl should be educated to at least 'A' Level standard.**

Well educated Jat Sikh parents from Jalandhar Distt. require a suitable match for their very healthy and handsome son, 26 years old, 6'2½" tall, B.Sc. Hons in microbidogy genetics from England, British National and willing to settle in Canada. The girl should be well educated either from England or Canada, homely, beautiful from a respectable family, should not be more than 23 years old and not less than 5'6" tall.

Matrimonial correspondence is invited by an Arora/Khatri Sikh boy of smart appearance. He is 30 years old, 5-6½tall and with Ph.D. qualification. He draws good salary and owns his private house. The girl should be beautiful, educated in this country and slim. Caste no bar. Inquiries from Jat Sikh/Ramgarhia Sikh families are most welcome.

Wanted a suitable match for a Jat Sikh 32 years old boy, height 6ft. He has been living in W.Germany for the past six years. Relatives lives in England. The girl should be holding a British Citizen and should be from a respectable family, Caste no bar. Divorcee can also apply.

and more particularly a woman, who is unmarried by the time he or she has reached 30.

When we compare the arranged marriage system with the Western attitude of "free choice", the arranged marriage would appear to be a brutal, inhuman system. But let us look at it a little more closely. The difference is not so much between Eastern and Western marriage, but between an agricultural village culture and an industrial city culture. So, for example, in peasant communities in Greece and Italy, you also find arranged marriages. Marriages in this case are contracts or alliances between families, and in such small communities there would be little or no choice in the matter.

In industrial societies such as Britain, the family has become much less important as communities have broken down. Also, individual members of families have become financially independent. A culture has grown up where the individual – not the family – is the most important unit. In terms of marriage, then, individuals are expected to be independent and to choose their own partners. Everything we see on television or in the cinema strengthens this view. We are continually bombarded with romantic images of people "falling" in love.

In the Sikh culture, the opposite is true. Each member of the family is seen, not as a separate

Dr Ratra and his wife, Parminder Kaur Ratra, just after their marriage in the Panjab.

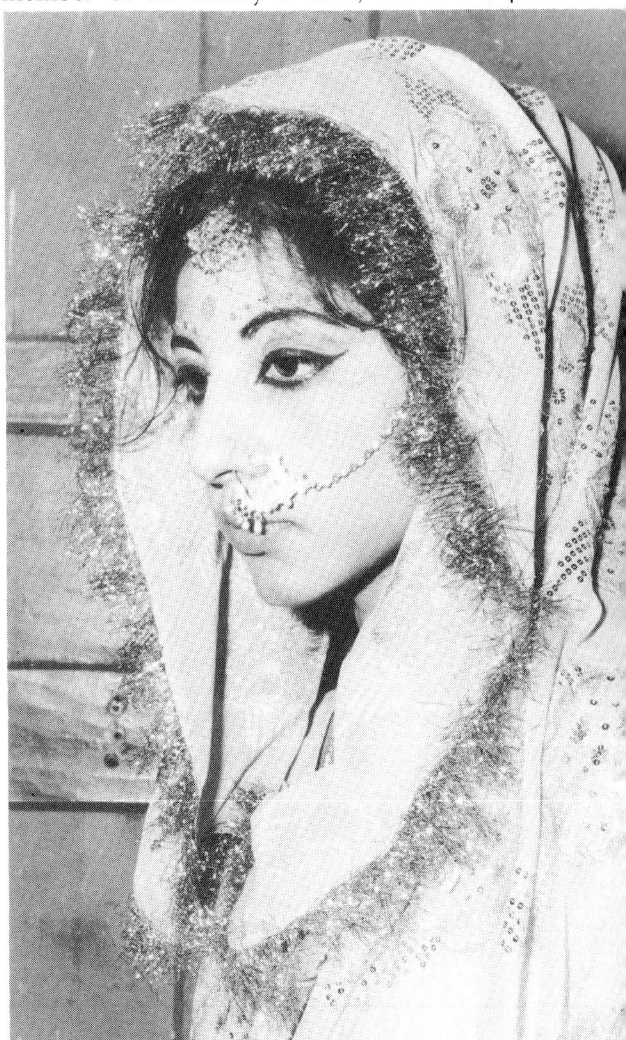

individual, but simply as one part of a family unit. Everything each member does is seen as being for the good – or the harm – of the family. This puts a lot of pressure on the children, because if they do something which is seen to be wrong, then the whole family is blamed. For a young woman there is the extra burden of pleasing her parents and accepting their marriage choice for her. Otherwise it would bring shame to the family and make it much harder for any younger sisters she may have.

There are a number of reasons for the importance given to the family. Most Sikhs are from a farming or village background. In such an environment, it was only possible for individuals to survive by working together in family units. These families would then work co-operatively with other families, hence the need to form alliances by marriage. In this sort of community everyone was dependent on each other, so the actions of one person would affect everyone else.

According to Sikh belief, being married is of utmost importance and forms the backbone of communal life. But it is not simply a physical and social bond; marriage is also regarded as a spiritual unity. In the words of Guru Amar Das; "It was vain to live together merely as husband and wife, they alone form a true pair who become one soul in two bodies." The Gurus themselves led the example of the Sikh ideal. Each one was a householder and lived with his family.

In Britain, there is another reason why families and whole communities stick together. When faced with hostility and discrimination from the host society, the only support and strength that Sikhs can find is within their communities and their own families.

So, despite the family being restrictive, it also provides a tremendous amount of security and support which young Sikhs often cannot do without. One young Sikh man who has left his parents' home explains the problems he faces; "When you leave home, you also lose a lot of support. It's like dropping into a void. I try and keep physically and mentally active. If I don't do that, I'm liable to sink into depression. I work during the day, and in the evenings I do a lot of sports.

"Living alone, and facing a host community which is very hostile, there is always a mental and emotional pressure. I react to problems in my life by becoming physically ill. I can see the political problems. I can see the racism. The fights and riots – all that is visible. But what you can't see and control are the mental problems that arise from those situations. Basically speaking, racism is something that scars a person for life."

Sikh children are growing up in a different environment from the one their parents experienced. It is impossible for them to adopt the same values. This does not mean that the new generation of Sikhs want to be absorbed totally into a British way of life. On the contrary, more and more young Sikhs are finding that they need to develop their own lifestyle and culture, drawing from both Sikh traditions and Western values. At the same time, they are increasingly questioning and rejecting certain accepted values of both cultures. This can only happen when there is mutual support – otherwise each person remains isolated within their own problems. The need for groups to provide this kind of support is slowly being recognized. For example, there are a number of Asian women's groups being formed around the country. Sometimes they simply provide refreshments and a place to meet for a chat. Others provide particular activities such as sports, or teach skills ranging from embroidery to making videos. There are others which offer advice and practical help on issues such as marriage, sexuality, race and women's work – both in the house and outside. Within such groups women are able to develop their strength and their own solutions to the problems they face.

## A Sikh Marriage

When Parminder Kaur reached the age of 18, her parents, Dyal Singh and Surjit Kaur, gave her a choice: either continue with her studies, or get married. Not wanting to study any further, she agreed to get married. It was decided that she should find a husband in India. So the first step was that her parents placed advertisments in Indian newspapers asking for a suitable husband.

A number of replies were received, including one from Ajay Pal's parents. Parminder and her parents then went to India to try and make a choice. They arranged meetings with each prospective groom and his parents. For Parminder, the biggest worry was the difference in outlook. She had grown up in Reading in England and her future husband would have grown up in a totally different environment in India. They were bound to be very different. This was, in fact, what she found with nearly all the men. "I looked at their photos first. Then I looked at their education and their background. I met a few, but they weren't my type." Ajay Pal, however, had already been to England and had worked in the Middle East. He lived a very independent life and she found his attitudes similar to her own. "At least he spoke English. The others didn't even speak to me. They spoke through my uncles." All these meetings had taken place in the presence of Parminder's father, Dyal Singh. After Parminder had told her father about Ajay Pal, a meeting with his family was arranged and, once the choice had been made, the relatives visited each other to confirm the new bond between them. During all this time Parminder and Ajay Pal were allowed to meet in

The groom, Ajay Pal, leads the bride, Parminder, four times around the *Guru Granth*.

the house but if ever they wanted to go out together they had to be accompanied by someone else.

To cement the bond, gifts such as household goods and jewellery, were exchanged between the two families. The exchange took place in December 1982 and marked the couple's engagement.

Parminder returned to England in January and, in November, Ajay Pal followed. They were legally married in a registry office in early December. To the Sikh community and to the families, however, the ceremony was not yet complete. There was still the traditional Sikh ceremony, the Anand Karaj ("Ceremony of Bliss"), which would take place in a *gurdwara*.

Normally, the new couple would not live in the same house until after this final ceremony, but, because Ajay Pal's own home was in the Panjab, he stayed at Parminder's parents' house. The Anand Karaj was set for 24 December. Three days before, Ajay Pal moved to Southall to stay with friends. The night before the wedding there was a party at each house, attended by friends and relatives.

Two days before the wedding ceremony starts, a continuous reading of the *Guru Granth*, known as the "Akand Path", begins. This is timed to end just before the ceremony begins.

The groom arrives first at the *gurdwara*, garlanded with flowers and accompanied by relatives. He carries with him a sword and an orange scarf. He sits before the *Guru Granth* in the hall, waiting for the bride. Outside, relatives and friends are greeting each other and exchanging gifts. Eventually, the bride arrives escorted by her sisters and other female

The bride's parents Dyal Singh and Surjit Kaur congratulate and bless the newly wedded couple.

relatives. She is beautifully dressed in a red *salwar-kameez* (Panjabi trousers and top), embroidered with gold thread. Her head is covered with a *dupatta* (long scarf). As she walks, the jewellery adorning her glitters and sparkles. She sits before the *Guru Granth*, by the groom's left side, and the ceremony begins. *Shabads* (hymns) are sung, and the Granthi instructs the couple on the duties of marriage. They symbolize their acceptance of these duties by bowing before the *Guru Granth*. Now the ceremony proper begins. This is called "Laavan" (Joining Together).

The father of the bride takes one end of the groom's scarf and places it in the hands of his daughter. This is similar to the Christian wedding when the father "gives away" the bride. With the other end of the scarf the groom then leads the bride four times around the *Guru Granth*. While they circle the *Guru Granth*, the Granthi reads marriage verses known as *laanv*. The *laanv* symbolizes the couple's spiritual unity, while the scarf shows their physical bond. Meanwhile, hymns are sung, and as the couple go round the last time, the guests throw flower petals and confetti.

After this simple ceremony, *Karah Parshad* (sacred food) is distributed, and the guests flock to congratulate and bless the bride and groom.

From the *gurdwara*, everyone will go to a reception at the bride's home or in a hired hall. Here, there will be speeches, folk songs and dances – there might even be a modern disco. Whatever the music, it is a time of frivolity and celebration.

Finally the time comes for the bride and groom to leave. Their departure is accompanied by traditional songs and dances. Almost by custom, the bride, her mother, and other female relatives will now begin to cry. This is the time when the bride will finally be leaving the security of her parents' home and will live with her husband. They will either have their own place, or more usually, will live with the groom's parents.

In Parminder's and Ajay Pal's case, they already had a flat to move to. Later, with the help of Parminder's father, they were able to move into a small house. They now live close to Parminder's family, and so they see each other very often. For them this is a successful arranged marriage which combines both the support and unity of the Sikh traditions as well as the freedoms of western life.

Ajay and Parminder a year after their wedding.

7

# Khalistan: "Land of the Khalsa"

Khalistan is the name given to the independent Sikh nation which many Sikhs are demanding. Although it has a long history this demand has become much stronger since 1984. In England there are a number of organizations working towards establishing the nation of Khalistan, and it is an issue which is becoming increasingly important in the Sikh communities. The recent events in India have led many Sikhs to take a much stronger interest in Sikhism and Sikh affairs. Many who had cut their hair have now started wearing a turban again. Learning of their history and of the treatment their people have had to endure, they have begun to reassert their own culture. Khalistan has formed the basis for a Sikh revival, inspired particularly by the teachings of Guru Gobind Singh. Yet, at the same time there is much opposition to the idea of a separate Sikh nation, both from Sikhs and non-Sikhs.

Here, we will look very simply at some of the events which have led to the present demand.

Jubilant supporters of Khalistan in Southall.

## The Fight for Self-Rule

Throughout their history, Sikhs have had continually to defend their property, their culture, and even their lives. Since the formation of the Khalsa by Guru Gobind Singh they have fought for self-rule. Or, at least, they have fought to free themselves from the oppressive rule of others; first from the Mughals, then from the British.

With the formation of Maharajah Ranjit Singh's Sikh Raj at the end of the eighteenth century, the words of Guru Gobind Singh, "raj karey ga Khalsa" (The Khalsa shall rule), had finally come true. The later loss of their kingdom to the British had been a hard blow to the Sikhs. Despite numerous attempts to oust the British, the majority of Sikhs, however, were content to lead a peaceful coexistence and negotiate for their rights.

## Partition and the Division of the Panjab

It was only when those rights were denied that they became more militant. In 1946, before Indian Independence and partition, Sikh leaders opposed the division of the Panjab. In general, they supported the idea of a united India, but, if the Muslims were to have their own country of Pakistan, then they, the Sikhs, wanted the Panjab to become their own state of "Sikhistan". This would join either to India or to the new Pakistan, but still govern its own affairs. Following violent clashes against Muslims, however, the Sikhs began vigorously to oppose the possibility of a new Pakistan. The majority preferred to have a divided Panjab and remain part of India, than to live as a minority in Pakistan. Yet, until the division was made, the Sikhs did not realize how much they were actually to lose. As a people they were to gain very little from Independence.

Even in the divided Panjab the Sikhs found that they were in an increasingly small minority. Also there was a tremendous revival of Hinduism. Panjabi-speaking Hindus were being persuaded to drop their mother tongue and adopt Hindi, the national language. They were even made to lie in the state census so that it appeared there were much fewer Panjabi-speaking people than in fact there actually were. These false figures were later used to undermine the Sikh demands for a Panjabi-speaking state.

It was an atmosphere in which Hindus were being favoured, and Sikhs were being discriminated against. The Sikhs began to feel that the only way that they could insist on their own language and their own culture, was by having their own – Panjabi – state. The government introduced two measures which strengthened this view. In 1948, some of the Panjab regions were merged into one unit – the Patiala and East Panjab States Union (PEPSU). The leaders, as well as the majority of the population, were Sikh. Next, the Panjab was declared a bilingual state with both Panjabi and Hindi as its languages. The Sikhs were quick to point out that, except in the region of Haryana, the spoken language of the Panjab was Panjabi. Also, most Panjab literature was written in Gurmukhi, the script used by the Sikh Gurus. "Panjabi Suba", as it came to be known, was a demand for a separate Panjabi-speaking state. The Indian government had already created other states with particular language majorities, so the Sikhs felt perfectly justified in their own demand.

However, the government realized that the creation of a Panjabi Suba would lead to the demand for an independent Sikh nation, and that the formation of PEPSU had already laid the basis for that. To prevent this, the government decided to merge PEPSU into the larger Panjab, so creating a state with a 65 per cent majority Hindu population. So the Sikhs were temporarily weakened by being outnumbered.

## Panjabi Suba

Under continuous pressure from Sikh leaders, though, the Indian government was forced to re-assess the question of Panjabi Suba. Finally, in March 1966, the government, under Indira Gandhi, passed a resolution to the effect that a Panjabi-speaking state was formed out of the existing Panjab.

To many Sikhs this was all they wanted – but others were unhappy. Despite making concessions, the Indian government still exercised a high level of control over Panjabi affairs. At the same time, some important areas such as the Panjab capital itself, Chandigarh, were taken away from the Sikhs and added to the Hindi-speaking state of Haryana. So, despite achieving some of their demands, Sikhs still felt that they were being discriminated against.

In 1984, a number of events occurred which brought the situation in the Panjab dramatically to international attention. On 3 June, the Indian government invaded the Golden Temple, the most sacred of Sikh shrines. It was an act which had drastic consequences.

## The Golden Temple Massacre

It is not within the scope of this book to unravel the enormous complexities of the causes and effects of the invasion of the Golden Temple. We can only provide here a very brief outline to help us understand the importance of these events to Sikhs.

The Panjab at the time was described by many observers as a "police state". It was almost totally under the control of the Indian police. Sikhs everywhere were being stopped and searched. Hundreds were arrested under charges of assisting or being terrorists. Reports abound of torture and atrocities being committed on Sikh prisoners by the police in order to extract information or confessions. Many were later allegedly shot and their bodies cremated in order to hide the evidence.

When we look at their history, we see that Sikhs have fought bravely for the cause of India. Also, in defending their rights, they have always done so firstly by peaceful means. Only as a last resort have they followed the words of Guru Gobind Singh: "When all else fails, it is permissible to use the sword."

After years of unsuccessful non-violent struggle, many have now done just that. They now see "drawing their swords" as being the only way to achieve their demands. Whenever Sikhs have turned to the use of violence, we can see it perhaps as a measure of the injustice they have suffered.

Sant Jarnail Singh Bhindranwale, a Sikh leader, had been using the Golden Temple precincts as a headquarters and refuge from which to mount guerilla operations against the Indian government. He had originally been supported by the government in undermining the Sikh leadership and creating divisions within them. Instead, he turned his resources to fight against the control imposed by the government. The government, under Indira Gandhi, in turn, laid plans for "Operation Bluestar". This was a seige and invasion of the Golden Temple, with the intention of destroying Sant Bhindranwale and his followers. The operation was executed with devastating results. The Temple was seriously damaged; the Akal Takht was virtually destroyed; and about 1000 Sikhs, including Bhindranwale, were killed by Indian army troops.

The Akal Takht shattered after "Operation Bluestar" by the Indian Army on 3 June 1984.

## Divided Reactions

The desecration of their holiest shrine sent shock waves through Sikh communities all over the world. In London, a huge demonstration of 50,000 Sikhs marched through the city in protest against the Indian government action. Charged with the accusation that Bhindranwale was himself defiling the Golden Temple by using it for military purposes, many Sikhs replied that their sixth Guru, Hargobind, had already set an example. He built the Akal Takht and used it as a military base. That, in fact, was its specific purpose – to be a centre of political authority: to resist tyranny and injustice by any means necessary.

An artist's rendering of the destruction caused by the riots in Delhi after the assassination of Indira Gandhi.

Yet this view is not held by all Sikhs. Some supported the Indian government's actions, or at least condoned them. With such a strong split in views there have inevitably been sharp divisions and tensions within the Sikh community itself, as well as between Sikhs and Hindus. But nearly all Sikhs are quick to stress that the conflict is not between Sikhs and Hindus. Many Sikhs look back at their history. They point out that two of their Gurus, Guru Arjun and Guru Tegh Bahadur, had sacrificed their own lives to protect Hindus. The conflict was not between Sikhs and Hindus, but between Sikhs and the Indian government, and Indira Gandhi, the Prime Minister, in particular.

### The Assassination of Indira Gandhi and its Repercussions

In November 1984, news arrived from India that would cause the tensions to erupt into bloody violence. Indira Gandhi had been assassinated by two of her own Sikh bodyguards. Once again there was a divided reaction. For some it was a time of celebration – the destruction of the Golden Temple had been avenged.

Khuswant Singh, a Sikh writer and journalist declared:

> The names of these two assassins (Beant Singh and Satwant Singh) will be read into the scroll of martyrs for years to come. It is the greatest honour for the Sikh to give his life to preserve the sanctity of the temple.

Other Sikhs however, joined in the mourning. They felt no joy in revenge, and denounced the assassination.

Whatever their opinions, there was an enormous and bloody backlash against the Sikhs. All over India and Delhi in particular, there were terrible riots. Sikhs – men, women and children – were brutally butchered. Sikh-owned shops and businesses were smashed and burnt down to the ground. The mainly Hindu police did nothing or little to prevent the slaughter. Some were even seen to join in. By the time the riots began to subside, it seemed that almost every Sikh family in England was mourning the loss of a relative.

There is evidence that Indian government ministers had themselves organized and stirred up the riots. What could have been their motive? To teach the Sikhs a lesson? to frighten them and keep them under control? No one can say for certain. And it is unlikely that the truth will ever be revealed.

Yet, whatever their reasons, the effect has been to create more unity within the Sikhs, and perhaps make them even stronger, even more determined. Many Sikhs are now convinced that they can never again live peacefully without discrimination and persecution under an Indian government. So the call for Khalistan – a separate Sikh nation – has become even stronger. As one Sikh observer put it: "It is not a question of whether or not we will get a Khalistan. We will get it. The only question is when."

Words of conviction, but the Sikhs in Britain, as in India, still remain divided. Many in fact are opposed to the idea of a separate Sikh nation and want to see Sikhs living in a united India. Dr Ratra, for example, feels that "the land of the Khalsa is everywhere. I remember when the Panjab was first divided, I don't want to see it divided further." Others, like the Singh family and the Phulls, feel no interest in a Sikh nation. Even if there was to be a Khalistan, they would not return there. As far as they are concerned, their lives are here in England.

Britain's Sikhs may be divided over the issue of Khalistan; they may seek different solutions to the problems in the Panjab. But, since the riots, they are united in their condemnation of the Indian government and its mis-handling of those problems. Until the government acts favourably towards the Sikhs, there will continue to be troubles in the Panjab. But, even if the government does start making concessions, for the Sikhs who lost so much in the riots it will be too little and too late.

# Afterword

In this book we have looked at the beginnings of a new religion and followed it through to its present struggles to defend and maintain itself. No doubt the struggles will continue; as one Sikh remarked; "Sikh history will always be full of strife. Wherever there is injustice it is the duty of a Sikh to try and overcome it."

At the same time, the Sikhs are a people with a rich and intricate culture. They wish to live peacefully and harmoniously with their neighbours, but are also prepared to defend themselves when necessary.

The Khanda, the emblem of the Sikhs named after the double-edged sword in the middle. Of the two *kirpans*, or swords, on the sides, one is symbolic of *piri* (spiritual authority) and the other is of *miri* (political or temporal power).

# Glossary

| | |
|---|---|
| *Akal Takht* | Sikh shrine and seat of political authority |
| *Akali Dal* | "Army of Immortals" – Sikh political organization |
| *Akand Path* | continuous reading of the *Guru Granth* |
| *amrit* | "nectar" – holy water for baptizing ceremony |
| *Anand* | "Song of Bliss" – a hymn |
| *Anand Karaj* | "Ceremony of Bliss" – Sikh marriage ceremony |
| *Babbar Akalis* | "Immortal Lions" – Sikh organization dedicated to fighting for Indian Independence |
| *Baisakhi* | harvest festival; also celebrating birth of the Khalsa |
| *bansri* | flute |
| *Bhangra* | Panjabi folk dance performed by men |
| *Bhatra* | Sikh caste (peddlars) |
| *Brahmin* | the priestly caste; highest caste in the Hindu caste system |
| *caste* | Hindu-derived social system, based on division of people according to the work they did; opposed by the Gurus but still maintained by most Sikhs |
| *chaat* | type of Indian snack |
| *chaat house* | restaurant/cafe which serves Indian snacks |
| *chowr* | a whisk symbolizing authority |
| *dahi* | yoghurt |
| *dal* | lentils |
| *Dasam Granth* | holy-book written by Guru Gobind Singh |
| *dholi, dhola, dholak* | side-drums |
| *diwan* | platform in *gurdwara* for the *Guru Granth* |
| *dupatta* | scarf worn by Sikh and Muslim women |
| *Five Ks* | *kes, kangha, kach, kara, kirpan*; symbols of The Khalsa |
| *Ghadrites* | "Revolutionaries" – political organization fighting for Indian Independence |
| *Gidha* | Panjabi folk dance performed by women |
| *Granthi* | one who reads the *Guru Granth* |
| *gurdwara* | "Guru's door/place" – Sikh place of worship |
| *Gurmukhi* | Panjabi script. Script of the holy-books |

| | |
|---|---|
| *Gurpurb* | Guru's remembrance day |
| *Guru* | teacher or religious leader |
| *Guru Granth Sahib Ji* | full respectful name for the Sikh holy-book, also known as *Adi Granth* ("First Word") |
| *Guru Panth* | Sikh community (organized body of Sikhs – "Khalsa Panth") |
| *guthi* | the hair knotted into a bun on the top of the head and worn under the turban |
| *Harmandir* | also known as "Golden Temple"; most sacred Sikh shrine |
| *Japji* | hymn by Guru Nanak |
| *Jat* | member of a Sikh caste of farmers and landowners |
| *kabbadi* | Panjabi sport played by two teams of men |
| *kach* | breeches; one of the "Five Ks" |
| *kangha* | comb worn in the hair; one of the "Five Ks" |
| *kara* | steel bracelet; one of the "Five Ks" |
| *Karah Prashad* | sacred food (sweet) served to Sikh congregation |
| *Kaur* | "Princess" – name given to female Sikhs |
| *kes* | hear and beard left uncut; one of the "Five Ks" |
| *ketha* | explanation of passage from *Guru Granth* |
| *Khalistan* | name given to an independent Sikh nation which many Sikhs are trying to form |
| *Khalsa* | "pure" – community of baptized Sikhs |
| *khanda* | double-edged sword; also symbol of the Sikhs |
| *kirpan* | small sword; one of the "Five Ks" |
| *kirtan* | singing of hymns, usually in *gurdwara* |
| *laanv* | verses recited during a marriage ceremony |
| *laavan* | "joining together" (in marriage) |
| *langar* | kitchen, where food is served free to any visitor to the *gurdwara* |
| *langoja* | musical instrument consisting of a pair of pipes |
| *Maharajah* | king, or ruler |
| *misl* | association of local Sikh leaders |
| *Mughals* | Muslim rulers at the time of the Gurus |
| *Panj Piyare* | "five beloved ones" – the original members of the Khalsa. Nowadays any five baptized Sikhs standing in their place |
| *Panjabi Suba* | demand for a Panjabi-speaking state |
| *Raj* | rule or kingship, government |
| *ramala* | silk cloths covering *Guru Granth* when it is not in use |
| *Ramgarhia* | Sikh caste of craftsmen |
| *roti* | flat, pancake-like bread |
| *Sabha* | society, as in "Singh Sabha", meaning Sikh Organization |
| *sabzi* | Panjabi word for vegetables |
| *salwar-kameez* | Panjabi women's tunic, consisting of long blouse and trousers |
| *Sangat* | congregation |
| *sarangi* | fiddle-like string musical instrument |
| *sari* | length of material worn as dress by Indian women |

| | |
|---|---|
| *sewadar* | volunteer working in *gurdwara* |
| *shabad* | hymn or verse from *Guru Granth* |
| *Singh* | "Lion" – name given to male Sikhs |
| *tabla* | finger drum |
| *takht* | throne, as in "Akal Takht" |
| *Untouchable* | lowest caste in Hindu caste system |
| *vir asan* | "position of the warrior" – squatting position assumed by Sikhs waiting to be baptized |
| *wak* | random reading from the *Guru Granth* |

# Useful Addresses

**Commission for Racial Equality**
Elliot House, 10-12 Allington Street,
London SW1E 5EH
**Institute of Race Relations**
247 Pentonville Road, London N1
**International Sikh Youth Federation**
P.O. Box 63, Darwell Street, Walsall WS1 4AX
**Minority Rights Group**
29 Craven Street, London WC2N 5NT
**Panjabi Language Development Board**
2 St Annes Close, Handsworth Wood,
Birmingham B20 1BS
**Sikh Missionary Society**
10 Featherstone Road, Southall, Middlesex
**Southall Black Women's Centre**
86 Northcote Avenue, Southall, Middlesex
**Southall Law Centre**
14 Featherstone Road, Southall, Middlesex
**Southall Monitoring Group**
50-52 King Street, Southall, Middlesex
**Southall Youth Movement**
12 Featherstone Road, Southall, Middlesex

# Book List


Muhammad Anwar, *Between Two Cultures*, Commission For Racial Equality, 1976

Campaign Against Racism and Fascism (CARF), *Southall – The Birth Of A Black Community*, Institute of Race Relations, 1981

W. Owen Cole, *A Sikh Family In Britain*, Religious Education Press, 1973

W. Owen Cole and Piara Singh Sambhi, *The Sikhs – Their Religious Beliefs and Practices*, Routledge and Kegan 1978

Surjit Singh Gandhi, *History Of The Sikh Gurus*, Gur Das Kapur and Sons (P) Ltd, 1978

Dilip Hiro, *Black British, White British*, Monthly Review Press, 1973

A.G. James, *Sikh Children In Britain*, Oxford University Press, 1974

S.S. Kalra, *Daughters Of Tradition*, Diana Balbir Publications, 1980

Race Today Collective, *The Struggle of Asian Workers In Britain*, 1983

Dr C. Shackle, *The Sikhs*, Minority Rights Group, 1984

Khushwant Singh, *A History Of The Sikhs*, Volumes 1 and 2, Oxford University Press, 1977

Ramindar Singh, *The Sikh Community In Bradford*, Bradford College, 1980

A. Sivanandan, *A Different Hunger*, Pluto Press, 1983


**Books published by The Sikh Missionary Society, UK (Regd.):**


*Introduction to Sikhism*

*The Sikh Symbols*

*The Sikh Bangle*

*The Gurdwara*

*Glimpses of Sikhism*

*The Saint Soldier*

*The Sikh Marriage Ceremony*

*The Sikh Woman*

## Picture Acknowledgments

The Author and Publishers would like to thank the following for their kind permission to reproduce copyright illustrations: BBC Hulton Picture Library, page 37; Indian Government Tourist Office, page 16; John Ogle, pages 3, 6, 7, 9, 12, 20, 24 (top), 25 (bottom), 27, 28, 29, 30 (top), 32, 33, 35, 38, 39, 40, 41, 42, 43, 44, 50, 51, 52, 53, 54, 60, and 65; the Phull family, pages 5, 13 and 26; the Ratra family, pages 30 (bottom) and 56; the Singh family, pages 24 (bottom left and right), 25 (top), 58 and 59; Southall Monitoring Group, page 61. The maps on pages 4 and 5 were drawn by John Ogle and annotated by R.F. Brien. The photographs on pages 10, 36, 45, 46 and 48 are from the author's own collection.

## Cover pictures

The colour photograph on the front cover shows the *Guru Granth* being read in the *gurdwara* (John Ogle). The background picture shows three generations of the Phull family as they were in Uganda (The Phull family). The black and white print shows Mrs Phull with her two daughters, Daljit and Manjit, as they are today (The Phull family).

# Index

**Numbers in bold refer to pages on which illustrations occur.**